Old Polish Traditions

T0275388

Old Polish Traditions

In the Kitchen and at the Table

Maria Lemnis & Henryk Vitry

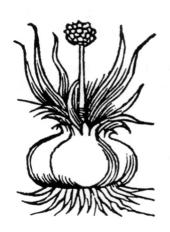

Hippocrene Books
New York

Originally published by Interpress Publishers, Warsaw.

Hippocrene paperback edition, 1996.
Eighth printing, 2012.

For information, address:
HIPPOCRENE BOOKS, INC.
171 Madison Avenue
New York, NY 10016
www.hippocrenebooks.com

Library of Congress Cataloging-in-Publication Data
Lemnis, Maria.
    [W staropolskiej kuchni i przy polskim stole. English]
Polish traditions in the kitchen and at the table / Maria
Lemnis and Henryk Vitry.--Hippocrene pbk. ed.
    p.   cm.
  Originally published: Old Polish traditions in the kitchen
and at the table.Warsaw: Interpress, 1981.
    Includes index.
    ISBN-13: 978-0-7818-0488-2
    ISBN-10: 0-7818-0488-4
  1. Cookery, Polish. 2. Poland—Social life and customs.
  I. Vitry, Henryk. II. Title.
TX723.5.P6L4513   1996   96-21627
641.59438—dc20   CIP

A cookbook?

Yes, a cookbook, only slightly different, because this one is in the form of a tale where typical Polish recipes are interwoven with a briefly outlined history of Polish culinary customs.

Much has been written about the Old Polish cuisine. Some criticize it for its reckless extravagance and for its excessive quantity of alcoholic beverages, others admire its unquestionable charm: its domestic intimacy, simplicity and abundance.

The history of Polish cooking had various turns, but Old Polish cuisine does not solely consist of the cuisine of the magnates, which absorbed enormous fortunes and which delighted in pomp and splendour and astounded with the quantity of dishes that made up a feast.

The true Old Polish cuisine consists of three culinary threads of the tale: that of the peasants, the burghers and the gentry. During the past centuries these threads either came closer together or drew farther apart, until they finally joined into a complete but differentiated and rich tale that included all elements of the Polish culinary style.

At any rate, the differences between these three threads were not, generally speaking, very clearly marked; in the cuisine of the gentry, for instance, there were great differences between the cuisine of the magnates, of the middle gentry and of the yeomanry, the last one differing little from the peasant cuisine. The rich man always ate better than the poor man. In other words, one can say that in the Poland of old there were several categories of cuisine (according to Zbigniew Kuchowicz, *Old Polish Customs of the 17th and 18th Centuries*, there were five in that period). These did not only reflect the degree of affluence, but also the tradition and culture of given circles and individuals.

In this process history also played a part, since dramatic and stormy political events and social changes had an influence also on what was eaten and how it was eaten. Therefore, let it not surprise the Reader that in our culinary tale there will be some mention of that great history which shapes all the spheres of a nation's life.

No monograph has yet been devoted to Old Polish cuisine. The subject is worth looking into, but it has not yet found a historian fond enough of it. This does not mean that it has fallen a victim of a conspiracy of silence. On the contrary, relatively much has been written about it. Many authors of the past and of today have touched on this subject in works dealing with either a separate historical period, or a chosen topic. This has enriched our knowledge of Old Polish culinary customs with very valuable chapters and contributions. The most worthy and at the same time the newest work on this subject is undoubtedly the work mentioned earlier, *Old Polish Customs of the 17th and 18th Centuries* by Zbigniew Kuchowicz (Łódź 1975).

The author of the first Polish chronicle, which was written in the years 1112—16, an obscure monk later called Gallus Anonymous, opens a long series of authors who in their works mention Polish dishes, banquets and culinary customs. If one collected all these Old Polish sources — fragments of numerous memoirs, countless epigrams, not to mention the valued culinary opinions and accounts of foreigners who visited Poland throughout the ages — there would be so much material that it would take more than the lifetime of one researcher to compile it into one work.

It would also be necessary to look into the small number of Old Polish collections of recipes that have survived in manuscript or print, e.g. the well-known *Compendium Ferculorum* by Stanisław Czerniecki, published in 1682, a work known today chiefly thanks to the fact that Adam Mickiewicz used it for reference when describing the last Old Polish feast in the 12th chapter of *Pan Tadeusz*.

All of this will most likely be tackled by scholars in the near or more distant future. Nevertheless, we felt we should refer to certain sources in order to enliven our modest little book on Polish cuisine with information and anecdotes from its glorious and long history. It is true that culinary customs are only a marginal aspect of our national culture, but this margin is so colourful that it is worthwhile looking at it a little longer, especially since it creates an unbreakable thread of tradition that links the most distant events with the present.

As we shall not even try to give a thoroughly exhaustive picture of the Polish culinary past, which would have to be put together like many thousands of colourful pieces of a huge jigsaw puzzle, we have decided merely to tell some anecdotes about this subject.

Polish culinary customs are not only confined to the diet typical of Poles. They are also the outcome of a vivacious national temperament, the famous Polish hospitality, sincerity, *joie de vivre*, open-handedness, sense of beauty manifested in richly-laid tables, as well as the attachment to and respect for tradition.

Many of us remember those tragic, sad Christmases and Easters during the last war: the raging Nazi terror, uncertainty of life, hunger and humiliating bitterness of the occupation. During those hungry Christmas Eves how comforting was that thin broth made from several frozen cold beets that ineffectively imitated the traditional borsch and the one herring, obtained with difficulty and divided into tiny pieces, which was to substitute the Christmas-Eve fish. How moving it was to share the Christmas wafer. wishing each other a Merry Christmas and remembering those who had died in the underground movement or had been tortured to death in Gestapo prisons. Similar emotions were felt during the sharing of the traditional Easter egg. Those were not meals, as they could not satisfy hunger, but patriotic symbols, making it less difficult to live through it all.

A new generation has grown up that knows those dark times only from stories and literature. For them Christmas Eve and Easter are gay family holidays that take place at a richly-laid table. May they remain so forever.

Also for millions of Poles scattered on all continents, who form a great Polish family abroad, the culinary traditions brought over from their country are something moving, maintained with care and passed on to younger people. Many times we have seen how a group of Poles visiting their home country from far away lands, upon carefully studying the menu, chose only the Polish dishes known to them often merely from hearsay. We had them in mind too when writing our culinary tale.

The gigantic food industry of the world, whose production is the object of extensively developed international commerce, has created a situation in which the cuisines of highly developed countries are becoming more and more alike, though so far this process is very slow.

At the same time we observe a growing interest in national cuisines, a phenomenon not without some sense. Thus the art of cooking has become a part of the cultural exchange between nations.

Cookbooks that contain recipes of various national cuisines are more and more popular, and so are restaurants which specialize in French, Spanish, Italian, Greek, Turkish, Chinese, Jewish, Yugoslav or Indonesian food. In this great international culinary chorus the Polish cuisine will certainly take a place worthy of it.

In this book we have not collected any particularly elaborate, ingenious or rare recipes. What we have chosen are recipes for dishes that appear on the Polish table very often, while not forgetting about cooking for feast days to which we have devoted two chapters — on Christmas and Easter.

We would like our recipes, chosen by us and entwined into a tale of Polish customs, to encourage readers to try them out often, thus continuing Polish culinary traditions.

Legend
and History

Man began eating from the

moment that he appeared on the face of the earth, and getting food was his most important occupation. Several million years had most likely gone by before man began creating what we commonly call civilization.

Palaeontologists have stated beyond a shadow of a doubt that the first groups of people were scattered in various climatic zones of our globe, which suggests the conclusion that these first representatives of mankind must have eaten differently, depending on the conditions in which they lived.

In those days time passed very slowly from our point of view and we shall never find out when food, which has never stopped being a necessity, started being a more and more skilfully administered pleasure. This happened so long ago that it cannot be dated precisely. It was only towards the end of the 4th and in the 3rd millennium B.C. that countries with a developed civilization, which included culinary culture, emerged from the obscurity of history, e.g. Egypt, Babylonia, and China. This was doubtless the period of the formation of the first "national cuisines", characterized by a considerable refinement and love of luxury. Of course, these are only more or less justified assumptions. Like the proverbial butterfly, products of culinary art are ephemeral and the first Polish recorded recipes are very young when compared to other written records. Handed down by word of mouth, just like folk songs, in the most part they have perished for good or were revived in an increasinghy perfected shape, keeping pace with the achievements in other cultural areas. However, some of these ancient dishes and drinks have surived until today almost in their original form, such as the now-popular roasted meats, kashas, cheeses, bread, wine and beer.

Old Polish cuisine developed on the basis of the cuisine of the Slavs. Unfortunately, the Slavic tribes that inhabited Poland in those days left behind few traces in ancient literature and even these cannot always be trusted. Polish soil, on the other hand, has been shown to contain abundant material relevant to Slavic history, which has only partly been excavated. These are authentic archives, priceless to a historian.

It is therefore thanks to archaeologists that we can get a fuller picture of Slavic, Polish history and even the chance to recreate in a general outline the everyday life of the people who inhabited these lands.

The Polish state did not spring up within a few days or on a land that was culturally barren. This is true especially of the Polane tribes, who brought into being a strong state that could effectively resist the attempted invasions of its neighbours.

Today, thanks to numerous and often sensational archaeological findings, we know that as early as the 1st-5th centuries A.D. tribes inhabiting today's Poland maintained close mercantile ties with Rome. It is true that the Roman legions never reached the banks of the Vistula, but Roman merchants not only visited the basins of the Odra and Vistula rivers, moving up through the many-forked "amber trail", but they also attained the Baltic coast inhabited by the Slavs. These merchants knew more about the natural resources of Slavic lands, of their customs and culture, than the great Roman historians with Tacitus in the lead, who drew their information about the Slavs from second-hand sources. But the careful and prudent merchants did not make their information public, if only for the sake of avoiding the competition of other "firms".

Slavic lands, the cradle of the Polish state, abounded not only in amber, which was extremely expensive and one of the strongest currencies in ancient times, but also in costly and much sought after furs.

Between the 1st and 5th centuries A.D. the importation of goods coming from Rome, Byzantium and even Egypt was on a large scale, as archaeological findings confirm. Not only have a great many Roman coins been found in Polish territory, but also many articles of luxury, e.g. artistically ornamented goblets, costly gold and silver jewellery, Roman gold medallions with portraits of the emperors, various silver, bronze and ceramic dishes, and glassware.

Even though the exportation of arms from Rome to "barbarian" countries was strictly prohibited, Roman swords have been excavated as well. Apparently the illegal arms trade is as old as the world we live in. Wines were also imported, which demolishes the theory that they appeared on the tables of wealthy Slavic lords after Christianity had been adopted by Poland. Naturally, in those days they were available for only the richest princes.

It is in those distant days of old that the beginnings of the Polish cuisine are to be found. This cuisine was probably more refined and diversified in the wealthier homes, as a result of foreign influence. But the original Slavic cuisine was, in spite of a certain simplicity, plentiful and not at all monotonous.

In the chronicle of Gallus Anonymous, written during the reign of Boleslaus the Wrymouth (1102-38), we read that Poland, "even though it is a country quite wooded, abounds in gold and silver, bread and meat, fish and honey, which is enough to place it above the rest; and although it is surrounded by so many Christian and pagan peoples and repeatedly assaulted by all of them at the same time and each separately, /it/ has never been completely conquered by any one; /it is/ a country where the air is healthy, the earth fertile, the woods flowing with honey, the waters full of fish, the knights skilled in warfare, the country folk hard-working, the horses sturdy, the oxen good for tilling the soil, the cows heavy with milk, the sheep with wool."

The beginnings of our history are marked by the grandeur of two feasts. The first contains a grain of historical truth under the cover of a legend. The second, totally authentic, with an exact date, was a feast of stunning splendour and with an unmistakable political character.

The first feast, a modest one, was organized by Piast, a ploughman of Prince Popiel, on the occasion of the ancient Slavic rite of hair-clipping* performed on his son, Siemowit. At the same time this rite was also celebrated in Popiel's manor. Two mysterious strangers knocked at the door of Piast's house, asking to be received, as they had not been let in at Popiel's home. Piast and his wife Rzepka welcomed the travellers with true Polish hospitality. The travellers, on their part, made the dishes prepared by Rzepka multiply miraculously, to the great surprise of the host and his guests. Young Siemowit, after driving out the generally disliked Popiel, gave rise to the Piast dynasty, which reigned until 1370 and the death of Casimir the Great.

Gallus Anonymous, when describing the hair-clipping rite of Siemowit, places the main emphasis on the miraculous events accompanying the rite, as these proved that the Piasts were worthy of taking the place of the Popiels. The author mentions culinary details by way of digression. We only learn that Piast had prepared a fattened pig, although the author wrote nothing of the way in which it was served. We can assume that Rzepka prepared other dishes as well. Gallus adds that Piast's guests washed the food down liberally with "a barrel of well-fermented beer", which was replenished each time, so that containers had to be borrowed from the neighbours. In describing Piast and Rzepka's hospitality, Gallus notices that "God does not hesitate to reward the hospitality of pagans even".

Gallus was a foreigner and a monk, and true Polish hospitality, heir to its Slavic precursor, did not escape his attention and is praised many times more on the pages of his chronicle.

However, the most famous Polish "diplomatic banquet" of the early Middle Ages that echoed throughout Europe was the feast given by Boleslaus the Brave in the year 1000. It took place in the Polish capital of those days —

* A ceremonial rite symbolizing a boy's passing under the care of menfolk and connected with giving him a name.

Gniezno — in honour of the Emperor Otto III. The emperor made a pilgrimage to Gniezno, to the grave of St. Adalbert, and while there discussed his long-range, and as it turned out utopian, political plans with the Polish prince. The plans were quite unusual for those days. The young emperor, a mystic and a dreamer, wanted to revive the Roman empire, which would consist of the nations of Europe, each possessing equal rights, united under the rule of the emperor as the secular representative of Christ on earth. Bestowing friendship and faith on the Polish prince, he wanted to win him over to his great scheme.

Gallus Anonymous describes the splendour of the welcome and reception in an unusually colourful way, presumably drawing on numerous other accounts, since over a century had passed since these events.

Prince Boleslaus "... had prepared wonders for the emperor's arrival: first, various troops of knights, then he posted dignitaries, like a chorus, on a broad plain, and individual troops that stood separately and differed from the rest by the colour of their garments. This was not a cheap and flashy display of ornaments, but the most costly things that could be found anywhere in the world... Having considered his /the prince's/ glory, power and wealth, the Roman emperor exclaimed in admiration: 'By the crown of my empire, what We have seen is even greater than fame would have it.' And on the advice of his magnates he added in everyone's presence: 'It is not fitting that so great a man should be called prince or count as an ordinary man, but rather he should be raised to the dignity of a kingly throne and his head girdled with a royal crown.' And taking the emperor's crown off his own head, he placed it on Boleslaus' head as a sign of alliance and friendship, and as a triumphal banner he presented him with a nail from the Lord's Cross along with St. Maurice's spear. In exchange for this Boleslaus offered him the arm of St. Adalbert. And so they were joined in such great affection that day that the emperor nominated him brother and collaborator of the empire and called him a friend."

Boleslaus acted like a true king. In his chronicle, Gallus Anonymous writes that the Polish prince, "for three days giving... feasts truly royal and imperial", showered Otto with many other equally costly items. He also presented numerous gifts to the emperor's attendants, so that "from acquaintances he made them the greatest of friends".

We do not know, unfortunately, what dishes were served on the gold and silver plates that the emperor received. We can only guess that they were excellent. Wine was also drunk, since Otto, who adored Roman traditions, without doubt preferred it to beer. Besides Polish dishes, there must have been also dishes served at the more splendid royal courts in other countries, with which Boleslaus the Brave maintained close ties and which surely influenced the menu of many Gniezno feasts.

Gallus Anonymous was not the only one who wrote of Boleslaus' hospitality. In the days of the Gniezno events it was also described, though less enthusiastically, by the bishop of Merseburg, Thietmar. Not partial to Otto III and particularly not pleased with the rise of Poland's power during Boleslaus the Brave's reign, he did not take part in the Gniezno celebrations. However, he knew the exact details from those who did take part.

Passing over in silence or criticizing the political significance of the emperor's meeting with the Polish prince, in his chronicle *Gesta Saxorum* he states that: "It is difficult to believe and describe the splendour with which Boleslaus received the emperor and how he led him through his country to Gniezno."

Referring to the coronation of Boleslaus with the emperor's crown and the presentation of St. Maurice's spear, the latter being one of the emperor's insignia, he notes with unconcealed indignation: "May God forgive the emperor that by making a lord of a subject, he raised him so high that the latter, forgetting how his father* had acted, had the audacity to subjugate those who stood above him."

It is not surprising that the magnificence of the Polish prince's court (royal court from 1025 on) in fact irritated Bishop Thietmar, especially as it was accompanied by political and military power.

King Boleslaus the Brave's cuisine was splendid, sumptuous and diverse on ordinary days as well. It had, in Gallus Anonymous' words, a domestic and Polish character:

"The court was kept so orderly and magnificent by him that with each day he ordered the 40 main tables to be laid, not to mention the smaller tables; and he never used anything but his own funds to pay for them. He also had his own fowlers and huntsmen from almost all tribes who, each in his own way, caught various kinds of birds and game and from each of these animals and birds dishes were brought to his table every day."

Ibrahim ibn Jacob, a Jewish merchant-diplomat from Spain, during his extensive journeys also visited Poland in 966. He described not only the wealth of the country, but also stated that during the reign of Mieszko I (c. 960—992) Poland was the largest and best-organized West Slavic state. The foresighted prince adopted Christianity from the Bohemians in 966, in this way averting the influx of German clergy. He also had influential ties with the German magnates as well as at the court of the Dowager Empress Theophano, the Byzantine princess. Boleslaus the Brave, son of Mieszko I, who received Otto III with such splendour, had spent some time at the court of Otto I as a hostage and so he could observe closely the ways that were then considered the peak of elegance.

We shall add that Mieszko II (reigned 1025—33), son of Boleslaus the Brave, married to the daughter of the Lotharingian palatine Ezzo, who was also the niece of the Emperor Otto III, was a ruler of greatly admired culture,

* Mieszko I.

fluent in Latin and Greek. Such splendid marital alliances must have influenced the court cuisine.

But let us leave these noble residences and return to the genuinely Polish cuisine, whose dishes were widely popular, as they were the inheritance of a long tradition, approved by the Polish palate. Food was served in peasant as well as wealthy homes in various more or less elaborate forms. Let us not forget that in the 15th century the crown peasants were still usually wealthy, owned many cattle and even horses. Sometimes a wealthy peasant lent money to the nobleman. Gradually, however, the lot of the peasants deteriorated, especially during the Saxon reign, until in the middle of the 18th century it was transformed into a wretched existence. The poorer gentry was not much better off then either.

Let us go back several centuries and look into the Polish pantry of the rich peasant or the moderately well-off nobleman who was an efficient farmer even though he might only own one village. As is well known, a well-stocked pantry depends almost as much on the wealth and hard work of the owner, as on the thriftiness and foresight of his wife, since the nobleman's manor and the peasant's farm were both self-sufficient establishments for many years.

The thing that will strike us at once is the variety of provisions. There would probably be several kinds of kashas, wheat and rye flour, peas, broad beans, hemp oil, dried and pickled mushrooms, salted and smoked beef and pork, frequently game, cold meats, pork fat, cheeses, butter, eggs, honey which was used for sweetening, mead, and wooden barrels of light, refreshing beer. We have enumerated the most important, fundamental products — and this list is probably incomplete. In this oldest Polish kitchen there was also no lack of vegetables, although their assortment was considerably smaller than today's. The list of vegetables eaten then included fresh and pickled cucumbers, carrots, fresh cabbage and sauerkraut — the old Polish favourites — turnips, garlic, and onions. Caraway and parsley were included in Polish cooking earlier than in Western European countries. In those days our ancestors already planted apple trees, cherry and sour cherry trees, plum trees and — somewhat later — pear trees.

Grape-vines were presumably cultivated in areas of suitable climatic conditions. In a description of Cracow from the 12th century we read: "It is a great and beautiful city with many houses and inhabitants, markets, vineyards and gardens." Traces of Polish wine production have survived, for example, in the names of some towns and villages (e.g. Winiary). The cultivation of vineyards did not develop to a greater extent, although Queen Bona (1518—57) tried to revive it. The cold Polish winters made it more profitable to import wine rather than cultivate vineyards. However, fruit wines were produced in Poland, which were less exquisite than grape wines, but certainly less expensive and of quite a pleasant taste, sweetened with honey.

Vast and magnificent forests provided great amounts of various berries and numerous rivers yielded different kinds of fish, which were smoked and preserved in salt.

Food was seasoned with salt, which was costly then and exported also to Poland's neighbouring countries.

We have good reason to suppose that spices appeared very early on the Polish table. Many ancient trade routes ran through Poland, connected with such centres rich in spices as Rome and Byzantium. The above-mentioned Ibrahim ibn Jacob writes that Moguntiacum (Mainz) was the centre of the spice trade for Northern and Eastern Europe. Having visited Moguntiacum in 973, he was surprised to see great supplies of pepper, ginger, cloves and other spices which, as he said, "grow only in the farthest East, although the town lies in the farthest West". It is difficult to imagine, then, that Polish housekeepers would not take an interest in this attractive produce, especially since it passed in transit through Polish lands.

Thus old Poland had things to cook with, bake with and

fry with and on the tables of the more wealthy there were dishes seasoned not only with salt.

There were also dishes, especially on the wealthier tables, prepared according to recipes from foreign countries, not only those neighbouring with Poland. Foreign merchants, when selling spices, must have also demonstrated their use. During stopovers, which were necessary because of the hardships and dangers of a long journey, they no doubt cooked for themselves using their own recipes. Thus Polish cooks had a chance to become familiar with more than one culinary novelty. Culinary art is an art which links nations and, as we all know, flourishes best during times of peace.

It is supposed that the Slavs learned bread-baking from the Goths. Bread played an important part in Slavic religious rites long before Christianity, which itself adopted much from pagan rites, allowing them to be merged with some Christian holidays, especially Christmas and Easter.

In Poland bread was treated with an almost religious reverence since the earliest days. If it happened to fall to the ground by chance, it was picked up and kissed with words of apology. Later, before a new loaf was begun, it was marked with the sign of a cross. Guests and newly-weds on the threshold of their home were welcomed with bread and salt. The great Romantic poet Cyprian Kamil Norwid (1821—83) wrote in Paris:

> *For the Land where a crumb of bread*
> *Is raised from the ground with reverence*
> *For the gifts of heaven...*
> *I yearn, O Lord.*

The popularity of bread in Poland is manifested in the numerous old sayings, e.g. "bread unites the strongest"; "bread cries when eaten for free"; "bread obtained through labour is tasty and filling"; or, the sharper in tone, "whomever bread harms, a stick can cure".

There have been and still are many brands of Polish bread.

Foreigners who visit Poland constantly praise them, declaring that they have retained the true bread flavour and aroma. The wheat-rye breads of long ago, baked in leaves of cabbages or horseradish — the so-called peasant breads — are an exquisite delicacy, although unfortunately less common these days.

Poles were great fans and connoisseurs of cereals, known as kashas. These "kasha traditions" also go back to the old days. One can write much and colourfully about the ritual importance of kashas in the old Slavic cuisine. "The feeding of the young with kasha" spoke of an engagement and "women's kasha" denoted matchmaking. In pagan times, when wanting to ensure a long and successful life to a newborn child, gifts of kasha, honey and cheese were offered to the goddesses of birth.

Polish housewives knew many ways of serving cereals. Thick, nourishing soups were cooked with them; they were eaten with milk, baked and roasted in an oven, flavoured with pork fat, butter, oil and cheese, seasoned with mushrooms and plums, served with various meats (it was some centuries later that potatoes appeared) and liberally covered with sauces. The Poles' fondness of kashas was recorded in the Old Polish proverb which said that "a Pole will not allow anyone to blow on his kasha", meaning that he will not let himself to be led by the nose.

The popularity of cereals started to decrease after the coming of the potato, but it has never been extinguished. Contemporary Polish cuisine still values highly buckwheat kasha served with roasts and especially with beef rolls, pearl barley and the refined, delicate tasting Cracow kasha.

The everyday drinks of the Slavs, and for many centuries of the Poles, were beer and the excellent meads. Wine was also known, but became popular much later.

Slavic beer was light, greenish in colour and sparkling. It was drunk then as we drink mineral water today, to quench thirst and during meals. In the beginning beer was brewed in each home for private use. For breakfast a kind of soup was served, made of beer, with cubes of cottage cheese or toast. The famous Polish beer soup, called *gramatka* or *farmuszka*, was very popular, especially in country manors, almost until the middle of the 19th century.

Many ages ago beer for wedding feasts was flavoured with hops, which were thought to possess certain features fitting the occasion. This is described in one of the oldest Polish folk songs, most probably of pagan times:

...If you, hop, did not climb on poles,
You would not make women out of girls...

Beers and wines were still the Polish national drinks at the beginning of the 16th century. The eminent Polish chronicler Jan Długosz (1415—80) writes that the Sandomierz and Cracow prince, Leszek Biały (1186—1227) asked the pope to release him from his oath of making a pilgrimage to the Holy Land, explaining that beer and mead was not known there and he himself did not drink anything else. This reason was so serious that the prince obtained his release. It was said, also, that Pope Clement VIII, during his visit to Poland in 1588 as the legate of the Apostolic See, became a great fan of the beer brewed in Warka. When, already as pope, he fell very ill in Rome, he demanded Warka beer in his feverish delirium, crying "Piva di Varca". The cardinals gathered by his bed, thinking the ill man was calling for the help of some saint, began to pray at once: "Sancta Piva di Varca, ora pro nobis".

The list of Old Polish beers brewed in various towns consists of dozens of names. The still famous Grodzisk beer was exported as far as Brandenburg. Other well-known beers were monastery beers and "noblemen's" beers, produced from jealously guarded recipes. Beer-brewing soon became a very important and profitable branch of the national industry. A very wealthy brewers' guild existed in Cracow as early as the 15th century, possessing its own tower in the city walls, from which its members defended the city during sieges.

We have shown a glimpse of Old Polish culinary traditions, as they are magnificent and deserve to be recalled. The later luxuries of the magnates make up another chapter in the history of Polish culinary art.

Here are several old recipes for soups made of beer and wine, and for some methods of preparing kashas. The hot beer and wine soups, nourishing and invigorating, were served for breakfast, less frequently for supper.

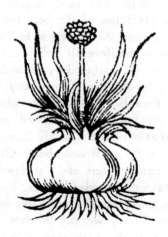

Gramatka or Farmuszka from Beer

This is an Old Polish Lent soup which was very popular, since long ago fasts were frequent and very strictly observed.

Into an enameled pot pour 1 3/4 pints light beer and cook with 4 oz. light rye bread with crust removed, adding 1 tablespoon fresh butter, 1/3 teaspoon caraway seed, a pinch of salt and 2 oz. sugar. When the soup is cooked, pass through a sieve and thin down with 3/4 pint boiling water.

Beer Soup with Egg Yolks

This soup will probably be more popular than the Lent gramatka, since it is milder and has the pleasant spicy aroma so highly valued in the Old Polish cuisine.

Bring to a boil 1 1/3 pints light beer with 3/4 pint water, 2—3 cloves and a piece of cinnamon. To this hot soup add 4 raw egg yolks beaten with 3—4 oz. sugar until light in colour.

Add croutons made of pieces of bread fried golden brown in 1 tablespoon butter.

Beer Soup with Sour Cream and Cottage Cheese

This soup was seen on Polish breakfast tables before it was replaced by coffee.

In an enameled saucepan cook 1 1/3 pints light beer. When the beer begins to boil, add 1/2 pint thick, not very sour cream. To this hot soup quickly add 3 raw egg yolks which have been beaten with 3—4 oz. sugar until light in colour. On each plate put some crumbled (or cut into cubes) cottage cheese that is not sour and pour the hot soup over it. Croutons lightly browned in butter may be served with this.

Wine Soup with Spices

This soup, considerably younger than beer soups, for many centuries belonged to the more elegant breakfast soups, particularly liked by ladies.

In an enameled saucepan cook 3/4 pint dry red wine for not too long (if sweet wine is used, add less sugar) with 3/4 pint water, 3 cloves, a piece of cinnamon, a slice of lemon or orange peel and 4 oz. sugar. Just before serving add 1/4 pint sweet cream to the soup.

Wine Soup with Egg Yolks

Cook 3/4 pint dry white wine (alternately apple wine may be used) with 3/4 pint water. Separately, beat 4 raw egg yolks with 4 oz. sugar and add to the soup, beating for a while without cooking until it foams.

Both soups may be served in teacups, with sponge cake.

Buckwheat Kasha

This is the most valued kasha in Poland, with a taste and aroma full of character. It is an indispensable addition (instead of potatoes) to all kinds of Polish beef rolls, roasts and gravies. It tastes marvellous also when served with plain milk, and particularly with sour milk.

"Toasted" buckwheat is especially valued. It is browned to a dark colour and has a more pronounced flavour.

During the ages Polish cuisine has passed through many styles, but the privileged position of buckwheat has not been shaken, either by the less nourishing rice, or even by potatoes.

Dry-Roasted Buckwheat

Pour 1 cup "toasted" buckwheat from which foreign substances have been sorted out, into a small saucepan where 2 oz. lard has been well heated. It is much tastier with lard than with butter. Roast, mixing, until the grains absorb the fat and are a little browned. Pour boiling water (1 1/4 cups), salted to taste, over the kasha. Cook over low heat. When the kasha absorbs the water, cover the saucepan and place in a medium-hot oven for 45 minutes. Kasha made in this manner is perfectly dry. Instead of water, a light broth made from mushrooms (dried) may be used. The result is excellent!

Fried Buckwheat

Pour 2 1/2 pints boiling, salted water over 2 cups buckwheat (not roasted) and cook over low heat until the kasha absorbs the water. Cover the saucepan and place in a medium-hot oven for 45—50 minutes. Place the hot kasha on a clean board moistened with cold water and spread evenly over bottom with knife, to the thickness of one finger. Place the board in a cool place, so that the kasha thickens well. Next day cut the kasha into cubes and fry in lard or butter. This is a truly Old Polish addition to a roast with gravy, since kasha goes well with all sauces, most of all with concentrated roast gravies and mushroom sauce.

Polish Krupnik*

Pour 3 1/2 pints water over 1 lb. beef and 1 lb. beef bones cut into small pieces and cook over low heat. After one hour add mixed vegetables (carrots, parsley and celeriac root, leek and 1 onion) and 4 small dried mushrooms. When the meat turns tender, put the broth through a sieve. Cut the meat into cubes and the vegetables and mushrooms into thin strips.

Cook 3/4 pint of the cooked broth, salted to taste, with 4—6 oz. pearl barley. When the kasha is cooked, add 1 tablespoon butter and mix the kasha for a while with a wooden spoon, until it turns white.

Add the cooked kasha to the remaining broth and after adding 3 potatoes diced into cubes, cook for a further 15—20 minutes. Now add the diced meat, mushrooms and vegetables to the broth and salt to taste. Sprinkle with minced parsley before serving.

---

* Barley soup.

Krupnik can also be cooked with pork bones, substituting beef with pork or 1/2 lb. lean smoked bacon (dice bacon into small pieces when cooked and add to soup).

Polish krupnik is not only very tasty but also very nourishing. If potatoes are served separately, garnished with onions fried in butter or only with fat and sprinkled with minced parsley, krupnik will constitute a complete dinner course, our appetites not being as large as they used to be.

Cracow Buckwheat Kasha

This is a very delicate, fine kasha obtained from specially ground buckwheat. It used to be the favourite kasha of Queen Anne Jagiellon (1523—96) and was regularly sent from Cracow to the Warsaw royal court, as the queen preferred the Cracow buckwheat to the luxury item of those days — rice. Cracow buckwheat kasha may be prepared in many ways.

Baked Cracow Buckwheat Kasha

Before baking mix the kasha with an egg. This is how to do it: mix thoroughly 2 cups of kasha with 1 raw egg, then pour onto a pastry-board and dry, taking care not to let the grains stick together (if they do, rub them apart in your hand).

Boil 3 cups of salted water with 3—4 oz. butter, add 2 cups of the dried kasha, mix only once and bake in an oven, in a covered pot, for 45 minutes.

When 2 tablespoons minced dill is added to the boiling water just before adding the kasha, it will have a delicate dill aroma.

A light broth from dried mushrooms may also be poured over the kasha, at the same time adding cooked mushrooms (2—3), diced as finely as possible.

In these three versions Cracow buckwheat can successfully substitute rice when served with e.g. chicken in sauce, veal ragout, mushrooms in cream, etc.

Royal Cracow Buckwheat Kasha with Raisins

Pour 3/4 pint boiling milk with 2 oz. butter and 1/2 vanilla bean (cut lengthwise) into 1 cup Cracow buckwheat which has been mixed with an egg and dried thoroughly. For a while cook the kasha over a low heat without mixing. When it begins to thicken, bake in a covered pot for 45 minutes in a medium-hot oven, as the kasha should not brown during baking. Having removed the vanilla, cool the kasha after baking.

Now beat 4 raw egg yolks with 6 oz. sugar until fluffy, adding some grated lemon rind if desired. Mix the beaten eggs thoroughly with the cooled kasha, adding 4—6 oz. raisins and then 4 very stiffly beaten egg whites.

Place the kasha thus prepared into a saucepan (or baking dish) liberally buttered and bake again in a medium-hot oven for about 40 minutes.

Place the baked kasha on a round platter that has been sprinkled with castor sugar and serve as a dessert, garnished with sour-cherry preserves. Sour-cherry juice may be served separately.

This tastes excellent when served hot or cold. Cracow buckwheat is said to have been prepared this way in the royal kitchen of Anne Jagiellon at the Warsaw castle. To this day this genuinely Polish dessert has retained its charm, untouched by time.

At the Royal
and
Burgher Tables

We do not know much about

the Polish cuisine of the Middle Ages as far as exact recipes are concerned. Numerous, but not very detailed writings say that Poles enjoyed meat dishes with plenty of fat, liberally seasoned with costly spices. More and more vegetables were used as well, and Polish breads were of a great variety in the Middle Ages, since in Cracow as many as nine different kinds of bread were baked. Dishes made with flour, such as noodles and dumplings, were still popular, whereas the consumption of milk, eggs and cheese was very large. The variety of cold meats also increased considerably. Next to hams and various sausages, many delicious small sausages called *circinelae* appeared. These could have been the prototype of today's frankfurters. Fish was often served, as a result of the numerous fasts that were strictly observed. Beer and mead were drunk, as wine was still an expensive and rare drink.

The greatest changes took place in the royal and rich burgher cuisines. Thanks to the numerous royal connections, close foreign ties and also because of wars, the Polish cuisine of the Middle Ages assimilated many foreign dishes, adapting them to the Polish taste and often changing them beyond recognition.

Cracow, the Polish capital of those days, took the first place in culinary novelties. The town was famous throughout Europe for its wealth, its magnificent royal castle, numerous churches, beautiful patrician houses, shops supplied with various costly goods, and first-rate craftsmen of different skills. With the establishment of the Cracow Academy by Casimir the Great in 1364 — which after Prague university was the oldest university in Central Europe — Cracow gained fame. After the revival of this school in 1400 by Queen Jadwiga and Ladislaus Jagiello, it became one of the most famous European centres of science and fine arts.

During the reign of Casimir the Great (1333—70), the last Piast on the Polish throne, Cracow entered the era of its greatest splendour as the capital of Poland, which under this wise king's rule became a very well organized state that had its say in European politics.

Chroniclers have noted that in his private life King Casimir the Great was a man of great charm. In chronicles we also find reprimands for his numerous extramarital love affairs and his shameful adoration of culinary pleasures. It is a fact that King Casimir had a lively temperament as well as a great appetite. He also enjoyed pomp and splendour and thanks to the fact that the royal treasury was well supplied, he could allow himself these things with a clear conscience.

One of the great events in Cracow during the Middle Ages was the "convention of the kings and princes" in 1364. This was a "summit convention" deserving to be described as such, and in its last stage it became a stunning presentation of Polish hospitality and the Polish culinary art.

This is how it began: the Bohemian King and Holy Roman Emperor Charles insulted the mother of the Hungarian King Louis, stating that she was "without shame". Such a serious offense called for revenge. But the emperor was stubborn and had no intention of taking back what he had said. Therefore, King Louis began to gather a large army in order to avenge the insult. The Polish king, Casimir the Great, Louis' uncle, promised to appear personally at the head of his army and Louis also managed to enlist the military aid of Denmark's King Valdemar, who was related to the Polish Prince of Słupsk Boguslaus, son-in-law of King Casimir.

Frightened by the extent of Louis' preparations, the emperor turned to the empire's electors and Austrian and German princes for help. A great diplomatic storm was brewing.

Pope Urban V grew uneasy as well, since once unleashed, war could grow to unpredictable dimensions. Therefore, he attempted to reconcile the quarreling sides and succeeded in this.

The Emperor Charles not only took back what he had

said, but set out to strengthen peaceful, friendly ties with the partners of the happily avoided war. He did this by asking for the hand of the Słupsk prince's daughter, who was Casimir's granddaughter and at the same time King Louis' niece.

The offer of marriage was accepted and it was decided that the wedding would take place in the capital of Poland — Cracow.

King Casimir with due ceremony invited the following guests to this typically political wedding: Hungary's King Louis, Słupsk's Prince Boleslaus, Denmark's King Valdemar, Cyprus' King Peter, the Margrave Otto of Brandenburg, Mazovia's Prince Siemowit, Opole's Prince Ladislaus and the remaining Polish princes. All of the invited guests, with the Emperor Charles at the head, showed up in Cracow on the appointed day.

An exact description of the wedding celebrations was given by the chronicler Jan Długosz:

"The kings were assigned special apartments and bedrooms in the royal castle, magnificently decorated with purple cloth, carpets, gold and precious stones. The remaining princes, lords and their servants were put up in magnificent inns that were supplied with everything for a person's needs and comfort."

By royal command the whole ceremony was supervised by the Cracow councillor Wierzynek, a burgher who had obtained his noble title from the king and who administerd over the castle and income from the royal estates.

Wierzynek, executing the king's order, displayed such generosity to the invited guests as well as to those who came "of their own will", that not only plenty of food was given to all and expenses were covered, but also everything was given that anyone requested for his own personal need and use. Let us allow the venerable canon Długosz to speak: "So that no one would complain about the lack of anything..., the Polish King Casimir ordered the Cracow market-square to be stocked with huge vats and barrels of the best wine and others full of oats, all of which he ordered to be replenished continually. From these the guests and invited persons drew not only for their needs, but also whenever they fancied."

The wedding took place on the third day in the cathedral at the Wawel Castle. The bride was given a dowry that was enormous for those times: 100,000 florins. After the wedding, knightly tournaments continued for many days — a novelty at the royal court — along with splendid feasts. Długosz says:

"King Casimir, wishing to show the wealth and affluence of his kingdom, treated the invited kings, princes and noblemen to elaborate dishes all this time. Furthermore, every day after each meal he sent costly gifts to all the kings and guests."

Councillor Wierzynek, who owed his great fortune to the king's favour, felt that he too should present himself with distinction. Therefore, he invited the five kings, all of the princes, noblemen and guests for a banquet to his own home on the Cracow market-square, where today the well-known restaurant "U Wierzynka" (At Wierzynek's) is located. The banquet was most probably financed by the town and Wierzynek received the distinguished guests in the name of the town council.

Długosz relates that Wierzynek, "with the consent of the monarchs, assigned the first place to his king, the second to the emperor, the third to the Hungarian king, the fourth to the king of Cyprus, and the fifth to the king of Denmark". The Cracow burgher received his guests with "elaborate dishes; furthermore, each one was offered magnificent gifts during the banquet". The most magnificent one was given to King Casimir, as the value of his gift (Długosz does not describe it more accurately) equalled the value of the dowry which Princess Elizabeth of Słupsk received from her grandfather.

The political aims of the Cracow summit assembly were fully accomplished, "the kings and princes, after strengthening their ties of friendship and concluding a treaty of permanent peace with a formal vow, and having exchanged gifts, expressed their gratitude and in turn praised King Casimir for the honour bestowed and for the gifts, all left for their respective kingdoms, duchies and estates".

Peace in Europe was saved (only for a short time unfortunately) and Pope Urban V did not conceal his pleasure. Długosz ends the description of the Cracow assembly with a sentence worth noting:

"In those times the name of Poland's King Casimir was famous and well known and from that time on his fame spread among all the peoples, and in all the Catholic and barbarian kingdoms the people praised the glory of his deeds."

The Cracow assembly of kings echoed loudly throughout Europe and the Middle East. Accounts of the Cracow celebrations are to be found, for example, in the rhyming chronicle of Guillaume de Machaut (c 1300-77), the eminent French musician and poet, published under the title *La prise d'Alexandrie ou chronique du roi Pierre*. Długosz did not exaggerate his description since the Frenchman, a visitor at many courts and himself an excellent artist, wrote thus:

"And how they were welcomed, honoured, served and received with bread, wine, all kinds of food and drink, fowl, fish and other meat it would be foolish to enquire for no one should ask such questions, as it is impossible to answer here how magnificently they were received."

Polish hospitality was renowned continuously since the memorable visit of the Emperor Otto III in Gniezno in 1000.

One of the greatest historical painters of the 19th century, Jan Matejko from Cracow (1838—93), created a colourful picture of the Cracow burgher's reception in the painting *The Banquet at Wierzynek's*.

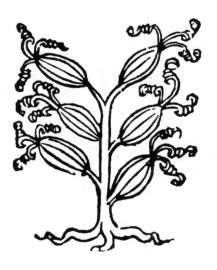

The Reign
of the
Jagiellons

Thirteen years after the death

of Casimir the Great (the reign of Louis of Hungary in 1370—82 was not marked by any great achievements in Polish history), his daughter Jadwiga came to the Polish throne in 1384. She was of the Piast blood, although not totally. When she began her reign she was only 12 years old and one year later, on the order of the Polish magnates, she married the much older Jagiello, the Grand Duke of Lithuania. At first glance this political marriage seemed ill-matched. Jagiello was a pagan and was baptized only when coming to the throne, accepting the name Ladislaus. He represented a completely different world that was far away from the splendour of the Hungarian court where Queen Jadwiga had been raised. Nevertheless, the royal pair, which began the Polish Jagiellon dynasty, distinguished itself in the nation's history. The king took part in the first great victory over Poland's enemy, the Teutonic Order (Battle of Grunwald, 1410), whereas the queen offered all her jewels for the reorganization and expansion of Cracow university, founded by Casimir the Great, which before long became one of the most famous schools of higher education in Europe, existing to this day under the name of the Jagiellonian University.

From the book-keeping accounts of the royal court it appears that Jadwiga and Jagiello had their meals prepared separately.

At the royal court everyday meals were modest and were not much better than those in the wealthier homes of the Cracow burghers. This testifies rather to the burghers' affluence than to the lack of it in the royal kitchen, which presented itself with greater pomp during special celebrations. Certain culinary customs became quite widespread; they were based on Old Polish cooking traditions and, as everything else, underwent a gradual evolution.

Queen Jadwiga doubtless had more sophisticated meals

than her Lithuanian husband. On her table there was expensive imported sugar and rice. She also enjoyed such spices as saffron, pepper, mace, ginger, cloves and such delicacies as raisins, figs and almonds. She kept these costly items in a jewel-box locked with a key. Imported spices were not a novelty in Polish cooking in those days and since the early Middle Ages they were often used in quantities that would seem excessive for today's taste.

We know a little about the way in which dishes were served. Among other things, fish in saffron sauce was considered a delicacy, as well as goose flavoured with almonds (we do not know, however, whether the almonds were added to the stuffing or to the sauce), chicken with stuffing liberally flavoured with raisins, rice seasoned with Hungarian paprika and so on. There were also various meats and game, roasted, braised and cooked, always in a spiced sauce, served also cold in spicy-sour aspic. In the queen's menu very expensive lemons were used.

King Jagiello, on the other hand, adored Lithuanian dishes and very hearty Old Polish dishes. Both enjoyed tripe and the specialty of Polish cooking — variously prepared *zrazy* (sliced or rolled stewed meat). During meals wine was served, most probably Hungarian, imported from the queen's homeland. Beer, which was inexpensive and widely used, was not ignored either. In Cracow many kinds of beer were brewed and brewers could be found on almost every street. Cracow's inhabitants of those times were connoisseurs of this drink. They did not restrict themselves to the numerous local kinds, but brought in a particularly valued beer from Świdnica and from other towns.

The Cracow market was very well supplied, as befitted the capital of a powerful country. When we look through the list of food products offered by Cracow's shops of those times, we come to the conclusion that even a contemporary housewife could make delicious and quite varied meals from them.

Bread in particular was of a great variety and of good

quality. Next to the various kinds of bread, "dessert" cakes were sold, with a filling of sweet cheese, flavoured with honey, poppy seed and spices. Numerous monasteries excelled in the baking of more elegant pastry, made in great quantities on the holiday of the monastery's patron and known as monastery bread.

Prices varied, but in general were considerably lower than in neighbouring countries. Even the great quantities of imported herring, the irreplaceable dish that added pleasure to the numerous banquets, were very cheap and accessible even to the poorest.

But for a repetition of the great "culinary festivals" Poland had to wait until the reign of the last two Jagiellons: Sigismund I the Old (1506—48) and his son Sigismund II Augustus (1548—72). Both of these kings were Renaissance rulers in the best sense of the word, great admirers of science and the fine arts, which reached the highest European level under their patronage. This was a period of the most splendid flowering of the Polish Renaissance, which developed on the culturally fertile soil of the Middle Ages.

However, let us go back to the times of the ancestors of the Jagiellon dynasty, during which the Old Polish cuisine began to spread to Lithuania and the Lithuanian to the Kingdom of Poland. To this day in Polish cookbooks we come across the expression "Lithuanian style". In the most beautiful Polish epic poem, *Pan Tadeusz* by Adam Mickiewicz, there is a colourful description of the "last Old Polish banquet" which takes place in Lithuania in 1812.

Judging by the dishes prepared Lithuanian style, the Lithuanian cuisine must have been exquisite. The famous Lithuanian ham, smoked very intensely, cut when raw into the thinnest slices, has an exceptionally noble aroma. With rye-wheat bread spread with fresh butter it was a delicious snack. From the numerous dishes originating in Lithuania the frequently praised *kołduny* (boiled meat-dumplings) have been accepted into the Polish cuisine, along with the Lithuanian *chłodnik* (a cold borsch), which refreshed on hot days and effectively sharpened the appetite. Only the origin of tripe, the dish so well liked by King Jagiello and his wife Jadwiga, is controversial. It was doubtless known for a long time in Lithuania and the Kingdom of Poland, but it was seasoned differently. There are many ways of preparing tripe, hence it is difficult to guess correctly which version is the closest to the "Jagiellonian" one. The dish is very popular today as well.

Tripe Polish Style

The preparation of tripe is very time-consuming and for this reason we usually eat it either in a restaurant or from a can or prepared from its frozen form. Tripe, when made with care at home, is a great delicacy and it is worth the effort to prepare it at home, if only a few times a year.

Buy 3 lbs. scalded and cleaned beef tripe at the butcher's. At home clean again, carefully scraping it with a knife, sprinkle with salt and brush with a coarse brush and carefully cut off the darkened edges. After washing several times in cold water, pour boiling water over it and cook for 15 minutes. Pour away water. Cover with fresh boiling water or previously cooked broth (which enhances the flavour) and cook over low heat for a long time, approximately 4 hours. Add boiling water to the evaporated broth (3 1/2 pints) continually. When cooked, the tripe should be so tender that it can be crushed between the fingers. Experienced cooks recommend the tripe to be cooked a day before its preparation. Cut the cooked tripe into thin strips and put into broth. There should be not less than 2 1/2 pints of broth.

In a saucepan simmer in a small amount of water with a large tablespoon of butter the following vegetables, cut into match-size pieces: 2 carrots, 1/2 medium celeriac and 2 fine sliced leeks. When the water evaporates and the vegetables are tender, add them to the tripe. Now take 2 oz. butter and 1 1/2 oz. flour and a finely chopped onion. First simmer the onion in butter and when slightly browned, add the flour. Be careful not to allow lumps to form. This can be done by mixing the roux with broth from the tripe. Pour this into the saucepan with tripe. Season with spices. Their proper dosage bespeaks the culinary skill of the cook. Add: 1/4 teaspoon ground ginger, a little ground nutmeg, ground pepper and pimento (allspice) to taste, 1 teaspoon sweet paprika, a small bay leaf and 2—3 heaped teaspoons of marjoram ground to a powder. Now the tripe may be salted (moderately!) and cooked over low heat for 20 minutes, in order for the aroma of the spices to develop and blend harmoniously. Thus prepared tripe should be of the consistency of a thick soup.

Tripe is usually served with meatballs. It is also good when covered with slices of black sausage or with potato dumplings. If tripe is served with meatballs, it should be eaten with bread. For those who prefer stronger flavours, serve tripe with small bowls of grated cheese (Parmesan), paprika, ginger, pepper and marjoram.

Tripe with meatballs is considered to be the most exquisite and may be served for a "Polish" luncheon. The following is a recipe for the meatballs.

Meatballs for Tripe

Chop 10 oz. veal or pork liver into a pulp with 2 tablespoons beef suet or beef bone marrow. To this add 1 raw egg and breadcrumbs in the amount needed for a consistency thick enough to form meatballs. Salt to taste and add 1 tablespoon very finely minced parsley. The meatballs should be the size of a walnut. Cook the meatballs with tripe for 30 minutes.

Tripe can be made more elegant by adding 1 wine-glass of dry white wine. But even without this addition, if carefully prepared, it is excellent.

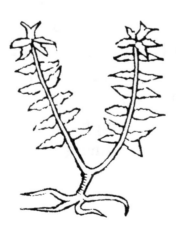

Lithuanian Kołduny *

This is one more culinary trace of the long Polish-Lithuanian brotherhood. They are tasty pierogi (similar to ravioli) with meat.

Begin by preparing the farce. Dice 10 oz. sirloin into very small pieces (on a board moistened with water) with 10 oz. beef kidney suet. The suet and beef may also be chopped separately, which is more sensible, and then mixed together well. Salt to taste, season with pepper and marjoram, then add 1 onion briefly cooked in broth and grated to a pulp.

To make the dough: Mix 10 oz. flour, 1—2 eggs, 1/4 cup lukewarm water and a pinch of salt. The dough should be thoroughly kneaded and should not be too hard, but flexible.

Roll out the dough thinly and cut out circles with a wine-glass. Place a knob of meat filling on each circle and form

---

* Meat dumplings.

small dumplings, joining the edges tightly, as the filling will expand during cooking and let out juice.

Place the kołduny into boiling beef broth. After 10 minutes of cooking, when all come to the surface, they are ready. Serve them in the broth, in soup plates.

The small kołduny are put into the mouth as they are, so that not a drop of the delicious aromatic filling is lost.

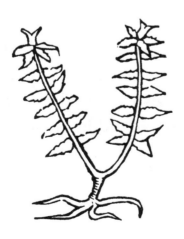

Lithuanian Chłodnik[**]

Chłodnik, also called chołodziec, is a cold, uncooked soup rich in vitamins, slightly sour in a pleasant way and refreshing.

There are several kinds of chłodnik, as it may be garnished in many ways. Here we present a tried-out and well-known recipe that is very simple and tasty.

Combine 1/2 pint soured beet juice (made by fermenting sliced raw beet and water) or the juice of freshly soured cucumbers (salt pickles) with 1/2 pint thick fresh sour cream and 3/4 pint soured whole milk (or buttermilk or yogurt). If only pickle juice has been used, colour the chłodnik pink with the juice from a finely grated raw red beet squeezed through muslin. 1/4 pint soured beet juice and 1/4 pint juice from pickles may also be used and the chłodnik may be coloured additionally if necessary. In older recipes it was recommended that cold borsch be added to chłodnik but

---

[**] Cold borsch.

this is totally unnecessary. Salt the chłodnik to taste and add a little castor sugar. The chłodnik should be mildly but distinctly sour. Now add 1 fair-sized bunch of minced dill and a small bunch of finely minced chives. A teaspoon of finely grated onion may be added as well. Add a peeled fresh cucumber diced into small cubes and preferably some thinly sliced radishes. If the chłodnik has been soured solely with juice from pickles, chives need not be added, but then the amount of dill should be increased.

Chłodnik has to "mature" in a cool place for 2 hours. One hour before serving place it on the lowest shelf of the refrigerator.

Place 4 quarters of hard-boiled eggs on soup plates and pour cold chłodnik over them.

Cold roast veal cut into small cubes may be added. The most elegant addition, however, is cooked shelled tails of crayfish. Unsuccessful attempts have been made to

substitute them with shrimps, but Lithuanian chłodnik and shrimps are two different worlds that are irreconcilable in
one pot.

Individual taste preferences are what de-
cides about the final flavour (as is the case
in most complex dishes). Some prefer
more sour chłodniks, others mild ones. Only
one thing is a definite must: chłodnik has to
be really cold.

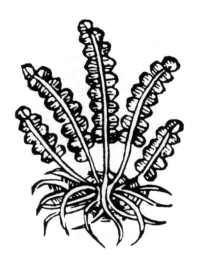

On Hunting
and Game
in the Polish
Cuisine

Hunting was a pastime of kings,

magnates and noblemen ever since the beginnings of Polish history. This was a true sport of knights, since hunting was usually done on horseback and Poles were known to be excellent horsemen during the wars too numerous for one nation's history, as well as during the short-lasting times of peace. Hunting for big game (bears, boars, bisons) was not a safe sport. The wounded animal often attacked the hunter, injuring or killing his horse. Thus it was necessary to fight the enraged beast even face-to-face, which required great physical dexterity, strength and courage. Many accounts have been preserved of Old Polish hunts that often took tragic turns. But the very moment of danger was what made the undertaking attractive. Aside from this, hunting developed fortitude, dexterity and alertness, all of which to a high degree graced the Polish knighthood. Ladies also hunted and they were no less courageous and dexterous than the men.

There was an abundance of game in Polish forests of the past ages. Bisons, elks, bears and boars were considered to be the noblest game, although stags and deer were valued almost as highly, especially on the table. Hunting for wolves and lynx was very exciting. Hunters also caught hares and numerous kinds of wild fowl, such as wood grouse, black grouse, ducks, woodcocks, hazel grouse, partridges, quail and snipe.

At the beginning fire-arms were not used and hunting was done with the aid of the bow and arrow, the spear, the axe and the hunting knife. The prototype of today's guns and rifles, the primitive Old Polish musket known as *półhak*, was very unreliable, since after one shot it became virtually useless. A second loading required a lot of time and the wounded boar, bear or bison attacked the hunter with lightning speed, forcing him to fight or into an embarrassing flight up the nearest tree.

Hunting took place most often with hounds, beaters, with

the use of a net (for a bear) and — less frequently — with falcons. Hunting with falcons was considered to be the most elegant form of hunting, but was also very costly. King Stephen Báthory (reigned 1576—86) gave two horses or three fattened oxen for a well trained falcon. Suitably trained hounds were highly priced, too, especially since during a hunt for the big game many of them were killed, mangled by the wild animal defending itself.

Hunting was an excellent training of the young for the art of warfare and an equally excellent means of preserving the physical fitness of their elders. However, with the introduction of the firearms, the immeasurable wealth of game in Polish forests decreased considerably, since with time there were fewer forests as well. An element which contributed to thinning out the forests of game was widespread poaching, which was difficult to control in spite of strict, sometimes even brutal penalties.

But even today, when the old hunts of the kings and magnates belong to the past, Poland is still one of the countries of Europe richest in hunting game, drawing numerous hunters from other countries and even continents. The French poet Jean François Regnard (1655—1709), who visited Poland during the reign of John III Sobieski (1674—96), wrote: "Toute la Pologne est le plus beau pays de chasse que j'aie jamais vu (All of Poland is the most beautiful hunting country I have ever seen).

Game is a valuable item on the list of Poland's exports. We also export live hares, in order for them to multiply in other countries, where they have been almost totally killed off.

Game played an important role in the Old Polish cuisine and no elegant meal could do without it. Today game, still very sought after by Polish gourmets, is seldom seen on tables.

Such Old Polish delicacies as roasted whole boar, bison and elk, bear paws and elk nostrils are described only in Old Polish literature. Deer, hares, pheasants, partridges, quail and wild duck, on the other hand, seasonally appear on the market, always finding ready customers.

Having somewhat whetted the readers' appetites, we present several recipes for dishes of wild game obtainable today. The recipes are based on Old Polish culinary traditions.

In Polish cooking the sauce obtained during the roasting of game is often enriched with thick sour cream (of the highest quality naturally), which discreetly enhances the characteristic aroma and flavour of game. This, in the opinion of gourmets, gives a better result than the rather more aggressive wine, especially if the latter is added in excessive amounts. Sour cream and wine, when used in appropriate proportions, complement each other very well.

The seasoning that is most often added to game in the Polish cuisine is dried juniper berries. They are used in moderation in order not to stifle the natural flavour and aroma of the dish.

Vinegar is mostly avoided in marinades, which are indispensable in the preparation of meat that has not "matured" enough or gained enough flavour. The usual base of marinades is lemon juice, wine and a suitable range of spices and vegetables.

Some of the favourite additions to game (and roasts) in Poland are cranberry preserves, beets and red cabbage (the last moderately soured with red wine or, better yet, with home-made wine vinegar). Rose hip or juniper sauce are the classic sauces for game.

Hare in Cream Polish Style

Having skinned and cleaned a tenderized hare, marinate it for two days in buttermilk that is changed each day. Remove membrane with a sharp knife. For this dish use the saddle and thighs, setting aside the liver, heart, lungs and perhaps stomach for a pâté, if desired.

Rub the prepared hare with finely crushed juniper berries and a little (1/3 teaspoon) ground pepper, then cover with vegetables that have been chopped into thin slices (1 large onion, celeriac and parsley root, carrots). The hare so prepared should lie in a cool place for several hours. After this time remove the vegetables, salt the hare moderately, place in an oven-pan and dot with small pieces of fresh butter (4—6 oz. in all, depending on the size of the hare). Add one dried mushroom (not more!) to pan. Cover the pan and place in a hot oven. During the baking, baste from time to time.

When the meat is done, cover it with
1 1/2 cups of fresh, lightly sour thick cream
that has been thoroughly mixed with
a heaped teaspoon of flour. The hare
should simmer in the cream for 10—15
minutes, so that the sauce reaches a full
aroma and good consistency. Divide the
hare into portions, place on a heated
serving-dish and cover with sauce.

This seemingly simple dish, when prepared
with care, possesses a truly exquisite,
delicate aroma.

Rump of Boar

The most refined and delicate roast of boar is the properly prepared rump. The haunch also gives a juicy and delicious roast. But if the roast is to be made of rump, then the piece to be roasted should not weigh less than 4 lbs. This should not be forgotten in order to avoid disappointments at the table.

Place the meat in a stoneware pot and cover with boiling marinade consisting of 3/4 pint dry red wine, the juice of 1 lemon, a thin slice of lemon rind, 2 sliced onions, 10 grains of pepper and pimento (allspice), 3 cloves, 20 dried juniper berries, one small clove of garlic, one small bay leaf, a piece of ginger (or 1/3 teaspoon powdered ginger) and 10—12 prunes. A piece of carrot, parsley and celeriac cut into slices, may also be added.

Marinate the meat for 2—3 days, the rump for the shorter and the haunch for the longer period.

In an oven-pan heat intensely 2 oz. lard and into this place the salted meat, drained of the marinade, and brown it on all sides. Now place 1 large sliced onion and prunes taken out of the marinade into the pan. Cover the pan and place in a hot oven. During the roasting, from time to time pour a tablespoon of marinade over the meat. After about two hours the roast should be just right. Now dust with 1 table-spoon flour and brown in an oven in an uncovered pan.

Season the concentrated sauce in the pan (there should be no more than 1/2 pint of it) with a tablespoon of rose hip preserve, a pinch of ground cinnamon and, if desired, a little sugar and salt. Thin out the thick sauce to its proper consistency by adding 2—4 tablespoons of marinade and rub through a sieve when cooked. It should be sweet-sour, spicy, but with the roast flavour predominant. Pour this sauce over the carved meat, which has been placed on a platter.

Rump of Deer   Lithuanian Style

The Polish-Lithuanian union, negotiated in Lublin in 1569, resulted in the formation of one state of the two nations, under the rule of a monarch who was king of Poland and at the same time grand duke of Lithuania. The union not only united the Kingdom of Poland and Lithuania politically for over two centuries, but also united them in the culinary field.

Numerous Lithuanian dishes have survived until today.

Having cleaned the tenderized, unmarinated rump of deer of membrane, salt it, dust lightly with pepper and rub with 5 finely crushed juniper berries. Let it lie this way in a cool place for one hour or more. Just before roasting, wrap the rump in thin slices of pork fat. This is better than larding it, as piercing the meat with a larding-needle means that it looses a lot of juice. Place the rump in an oven-pan, cover liberally with melted butter (2—3 oz.) and roast in a medium-hot oven. When the pork fat wrapped around the rump browns nicely, remove it to the side and dust the rump several times with a little castor sugar (1 oz.). The sugar, melting in high temperature, will form a golden brown appetizing crisp caramel coating on the surface of the rump. Not only the external effect is important: the meat gains in flavour under the influence of the sugar.

When the rump is roasted, beat 1 1/2 cups of fresh thick cream with a heaped teaspoon of flour and the juice of 2 small lemons. Salt the sauce to taste and cook briefly, then pour into the pan, from which the pork fat has been removed. When the sauce starts to boil again, take out the meat and add 3 oz. butter divided into small pieces to the sauce. Do not cook the sauce again, but for a while beat it in the pan with a whisk and pour over the meat, which has been divided into portions and arranged on a platter. The sauce must be hot.

Roast Pheasant

The pheasant (the females have much tastier and more tender meat) should be suitably tenderized. Therefore, after it has been hunted, it should be hung "in its feathers" in a cool place for 5—6 days. After this time pluck the bird of its feathers when dry, draw it, quickly rinse the inside and outside and dry with a clean linen cloth.

Mince the liver and heart to a pulp and cream with 2 oz. butter, then salt to taste, adding a teaspoon of lemon juice while creaming. We recommend the addition of 5 finely crushed (in a mortar) dried juniper berries. Cover the inside of the bird evenly with this paste.

Rub the bird with salt moderately, then wrap it in thin slices of pork fat, place in an oven-pan in which a tablespoon of fresh butter has been melted. Bake in an oven. 10 minutes before taking the meat out of the oven, remove the pork fat so that the pheasant's skin browns nicely, but not too much.

Thin down the concentrated sauce in the pan by mixing with 2 tablespoons broth or a mixture of 1/2 part broth to 1/2 part dry white wine. Cook for a while and, while still hot, pour over the pheasant, which has been divided into portions and arranged on a heated platter.

An excellent addition to this dish is bilberry preserves with a little lemon juice if desired.

Roast Partridges and Quail

Young roasted partridges are delicate and elegant dishes that are unfortunately rare. They are prepared in various ways. We present a recipe that is unusually easy and in spite of this retains the birds' natural taste and aroma.

Having removed the feathers completely and drawn the partridges (quail), wash the birds briefly under cold running water and dry thoroughly. Salt moderately inside and outside, then wrap each bird individually in thin slices of pork fat and tie with scalded cotton thread. 2—3 sage leaves placed inside each partridge enhance the flavour of the meat considerably.

Roast partridges thus prepared on a roasting spit or in an oven, basting them with a teaspoon of melted butter from time to time while roasting.

Having removed the thread, place the roasted partridges on warm toasts made of bread lightly browned in butter. Thin down the sauce which has formed during roasting with 2 tablespoons broth and pour over the birds. The jacket of attractively browned pork fat may be left on the partridges, as it has a very good flavour.

Juniper Sauce

Chop leftover game into very small pieces (2 tablespoons), add 2 oz. smoked bacon, 1 finely chopped onion, 1 tablespoon dried juniper berries, 1/2 finely chopped carrot and 1/4 finely chopped celeriac. Simmer all this in a saucepan. When vegetables begin to brown lightly, add 1 cup broth and cook over low heat for one hour, adding some broth if necessary.

Lightly brown 1 oz. flour in 1 oz. butter, add the vegetables with juniper, cook and rub through a sieve. Now add 1/2 cup dry white wine, salt to taste and if the sauce seems too bland for you, season to taste with lemon juice.

A teaspoon of good tomato paste may also be added to enliven the flavour.

Juniper sauce is widely used in Polish cooking. It is added to roast game, pork and lamb (an excellent combination!) and to pâtés that are served hot.

When There Is no Game on Hand...

Today game is a rare delicacy that is slowly disappearing and becoming more expensive. However, there is a way, discovered long ago, to give non-game meats a characteristic flavour and aroma sometimes almost totally like that of game. This is achieved with the aid of appropriately composed marinades and seasoning, especially with dried juniper berries.

The following are some examples of very tasty meat dishes with the flavour and aroma of game so cherished by gourmets.

Roast Pork Wild Game Style

This carefully prepared roast, very successfully imitating roast boar, is even more tender and juicy than boar.

Place 3 lbs. lean pork for the roast in a stoneware pot. Make marinade from 1/2 cup dry white wine, the juice of 1 large lemon, 20 lightly crushed dried juniper berries, 10 grains pepper, 10 grains pimento (allspice), 2 cloves and 1 bay leaf. Cook all these ingredients and pour over the meat, which should be marinated for 4 days in a cool place. Since there is little marinade, the meat should be turned over twice a day. Before pouring marinade, place 2 sliced onions on the meat.

After taking meat out of marinade, rub it with salt and leave for one hour in a cool place. Now fry the meat in 2 oz. intensely heated lard until browned, place in an oven, slowly roasting in medium heat. During the roasting baste it with its own sauce from time to time. After 1 hour of roasting add 1 large sliced onion. When the meat becomes tender, sprinkle 1 teaspoon flour into the sauce in pan. Put the marinade from the meat through a sieve, then pour it into the sauce. After a while add 1 tablespoon rose hip preserve (which has the most "style"; if not available, 1 tablespoon cherry jam may be used) and 1 1/2 cups of broth. The sauce should barely simmer for 10 minutes. Carve the meat into slices and pour the sauce over it.

Dry-roasted buckwheat kasha is the best addition to this roast pork, as well as the "classic" Polish beets, which may be flavoured with sour cream.

Roast Beef Wild Game Style

This is an excellent dish hot or cold. Tartar sauce or ketchup may be added when served cold. Take a neatly cut piece of meat for the roast (2—3 lbs.), pour marinade over it, made from finely diced vegetables: 1/2 carrot, parsley root, 1/2 medium celeriac, small bay leaf, 10 grains pepper and pimento (allspice), a pinch of dried thyme, 10 lightly crushed dried juniper berries, 2 sliced onions, the juice of 1 1/2 lemons and 4 tablespoons water. It is advisable, but not necessary, to add one wineglass of dry red wine. Cook the above ingredients briefly and pour the boiling liquid over the meat, which has been placed in a porcelain dish or stoneware pot. After two days (keep the meat in a cool place, turning it over from time to time in order for it to soak thoroughly), take the meat out of the marinade and rub with salt (one hour before roasting), lard with pork fat, dust lightly (1/2 teaspoon) with paprika and place in an oven-pan in very hot fat (c. 2 oz. lard). When the meat browns nicely on all sides, add the vegetables and spices from the marinade. Place the covered pan in an oven and from time to time pour alternately 1 tablespoon water and 1 tablespoon marinade and then its own sauce over it.

Over the tender roast pour 3/4 cup thick sour cream, which has been thoroughly mixed with 1 heaped teaspoon wheat flour. The sauce should boil only once, afterwards it should simmer over low heat for 2—3 minutes.

Cut the roast into not too thin slices (when cold — very thin slices!) and cover with the sauce, which has been put through a sieve. The sauce should be seasoned to taste (salt may be added, a pinch of sugar or some lemon juice).

The most suitable addition to this roast is home-made noodles. As a vegetable, traditional beets may be served, this time not flavoured with sour cream.

If the roast is to be served cold, do not flavour it with sour cream.

Roast veal wild game style is prepared in a similar way, the only difference being that butter instead of lard is used. Also, the meat is larded or wrapped and tied in pork fat and wine is not added to the marinade.

Duck Wild Game Style

Among domestic birds only ducks can be successfully prepared "wild game style". Since the duck is marinated before roasting, an older bird may be used, as it becomes tender in the marinade. The duck should be lean, as fatted birds are not suitable for this version.

The marinade is made from 1/2 cup dry red wine, the juice and piece of rind of a large lemon, 5 grains of pepper and pimento (allspice), 10 lightly crushed juniper berries, 3 cloves, a piece of ginger or 1/2 teaspoon powdered ginger, finely diced vegetables (1/2 carrot, 1/2 parsley root, 1/4 celeriac), 1 sliced onion, 1 bay leaf and 1 cup water. Pour boiling water over the vegetables and onion, cook for 30 minutes, then add spices, wine, lemon juice and a small thin slice of lemon rind. Cook briefly once more and pour cool marinade over the thoroughly cleaned duck. Older ducks are marinated for three days, younger ones only two. During the marinating process, turn the bird over from time to time in order for the marinade to soak through well and to give the meat flavour.

One hour before roasting salt the duck, then roast slowly in a pan in butter (2 oz.). While roasting, baste the bird with the sauce formed in the pan. When the meat becomes tender, remove the duck from the pan and divide into portions.

Carefully remove 2—3 tablespoons of fat from the sauce, add 1 level teaspoon sugar and, mixing, fry the fat until the sugar is lightly browned. Then add 1 level tablespoon flour and, having browned it quickly, thin down with 1/2 cup broth, combine with the sauce in pan and add the marinade with spices and vegetables to taste. The sauce should be spicy and have a distinct, pungent, gamy taste. After 2 minutes of cooking pour the strained sauce over the duck, heat to boiling point and serve on a platter with sauce over it. Serve with home-made noodles or dry-roasted rice.

We present these three "wild game style" recipes with the numerous fans of wild game in mind who are not hunters and do not have a hunter in the family. The dishes are popular in the Polish cuisine and, when prepared with care, are a good substitute for the game that is so difficult to obtain nowadays. Since game tastes best in autumn and in winter, we suggest that "wild game style" dishes be prepared at these times of the year.

On
Mushrooms

In Polish forests, shrubs and

meadows there is a variety of edible mushrooms. Thus, experienced mushroom pickers have something to choose from during the long mushroom season, as there are 31 kinds of mushrooms officially recognized as edible by the Ministry of Health and Social Welfare. Unofficially there are more, but these are types which appear only sporadically in certain areas and hence are known locally, especially in folk cuisine.

Mushrooms, if not solely associated with the frying pan and saucepan, are a true feast for the eyes. The very act of picking them, even if not many are picked, is so pleasant a relaxation for big city inhabitants, that it can only be compared to the noble sport of fishing on quiet lakes. The unusual wealth of shape and colour of mushrooms growing in emerald-green moss or against the subdued russet background of fallen leaves sometimes creates fantastic and picturesque constellations, deserving to be compared with flowers. This feature has not been ignored by Polish poets who, paying just homage to the beauty of mushrooms, have not forgotten their culinary virtues.

The following is the most beautiful and famous poetical description of mushroom picking in Polish literature, in *Pan Tadeusz* by Adam Mickiewicz:

> *Mushrooms were plentiful: the boys preferred*
> *The vixens (that's the Lithuanian word)*
> *Emblems of maidenhood; uneat by worms,*
> *No insect ever lights upon their forms.*
> *The girls the slender forester pursued,*
> *In song called colonel of the mushroom brood.*
> *All sought the orange agaric, less tall*
> *And famed in song, but tastiest of all,*
> *Or salt or fresh, and good in any season.*
> *The Seneschal picked flybane — for reason.*
> *The other kinds of mushroom are not favoured,*
> *Because they're harmful or are evil-flavoured.*

They are not useless but for beasts are good,
Shelter the insects and adorn the wood.
They stand upon the grassy cloth in order
Like rows of plates: such as with scalloped border
The small leaf mushrooms, silver, red and gold
Like goblets that all kinds of liquor hold;
The kids like swelling cups turned upside down;
The funnels slim like champagne glasses grown;
The kind called white that broad and flattish gleam
Like china coffee cups filled full of cream... *

Polish cuisine owes much to mushrooms. Since the earliest days they have been the base for many typically Polish dishes. Today, when the forests have been thinned out so much, there are also fewer mushrooms, particularly as they are extremely sensitive to external factors such as air pollution, and also very capricious. There are years of plenty when forests abound in mushrooms, equally as hard to predict as bad years when mushrooms are scarce. Attempts to "domesticate"the noblest and most sought after Polish mushroom, the boletus *(Boletus edulis)*, have failed and it cannot be grown in the manner of the common white field mushroom or champignon.

There are more and more fans of mushrooms. And this is the reason why mushrooms, especially dried boletus (in Polish called real mushrooms), have become a delicacy that is expensive yet in demand on world markets.

Poland is still a "mine of mushrooms" when compared to most other European countries and Polish mushrooms are famous the world over.

In Old Polish kitchens they were prepared in various ways, as a main course, as an hours d'oeuvre, and as an aromatic addition to many sauces and soups. For example, usually

* Adam Mickiewicz: *Pan Tadeusz or the Last Foray in Lithuania — A Tale of the Gentry in the Years 1811 and 1812*, translated into English Verse with an introduction by Kenneth Mackenzie. The Polish Cultural Foundation, London 1964, Caldra House Ltd., 23 Coleridge Street, Hove 3, Sussex.

only one mushroom was added to broth, 2—3 mushrooms to *grochówka* (pea soup) and *kapuśniak* (cabbage soup), whereas not less than a handful was added to the Christmas Eve borsch.

They were also an irreplaceable addition to many roasts, to game, poultry and certain fish dishes, to cabbage, *bigos* and many other Old Polish dishes. Often only one dried mushroom saved a soup or sauce that lacked taste, since culinary success depends not on the amount of mushrooms, but on hitting the right dosage. It can be said without exaggeration that the noble aroma of mushrooms, sometimes barely discernible, has wound its way through hundreds of dishes like a golden thread, giving them their uniquely Polish character.

In the 18th century, along with the growing influence of French cuisine, champignons appeared at the tables of magnates and at King Stanislaus Augustus' elegant dinners. They were quite expensive at first. With time, when their easy cultivation had been learnt, they made themselves at home for good in the Polish cuisine. Today champignons, relatively inexpensive and available the year round, are a good supplement to the variety of "Polish mushrooms", especially as the years when mushrooms are scarce are unfortunately quite frequent.

Hot Snack from Dried Mushrooms

Pour cold milk over fine, not too large caps of boletus mushrooms (3 caps per person), so that the mushrooms are barely covered, and leave overnight. Next day add some water to the milk and cook mushrooms until soft. Drain and cool the caps, then salt lightly and add some pepper, dip in flour, beaten egg and finely sifted breadcrumbs.

Fry the coated mushrooms on both sides in butter until nicely browned. Serve in the pan in which they were fried, garnished with parsley sprigs fried in butter.

This is an Old Polish winter snack, served with dry Polish vodkas.

Fresh Mushroom Soup

Take 1 lb. fresh boletus mushrooms (or various edible mushrooms) that have been cleaned of sand and rinsed in cold water. Cut into thin slices and dice finely the stems, making sure none are worm-eaten. Melt one heaped tablespoon of butter in a saucepan, add the mushrooms and one finely diced onion, and fry over medium heat until onion and mushrooms brown slightly.

Pour vegetable broth or thin chicken soup (2 1/4 pints) over the mushrooms, cook and either add 1 tablespoon flour which has been browned in 1 tablespoon butter, or, for a change, add 1/4 pint sour cream to soup. After adding the roux cook the soup briefly and on adding the cream heat intensely, but only until soup reaches boiling point. Salt to taste and add lemon juice if desired.

Łazanki (a kind of noodles) or noodles made from blintzes formed into a roll and sliced thinly (3 blintzes) are added to this soup.

Duck Cracow Style with Mushrooms

Clean a fine, lean duck thoroughly and, having salted it, stew in a pan in butter with 1 medium thinly sliced onion, from time to time pouring broth made from dried mushrooms over it.

In order to obtain a very aromatic broth, pour 3/4 pint water over 2 oz. dried mushrooms and cook, covered, over low heat until tender.

First fry the duck in a small amount of fat (or in oil or lard) over high heat, so that the bird browns nicely. When it does, reduce the heat and stew the duck, covered, from time to time pouring mushroom broth over it. When the duck is tender, remove it from the pan and, when somewhat cooler, divide into 4—6 portions.

Mix thoroughly 1/2 pint sour cream with an almost heaped teaspoon flour. Add this to the sauce remaining in the pan. Add finely diced mushrooms to the sauce and pour it over the duck portions. Place the pan over low heat again and allow the sauce to simmer lightly for 10 minutes.

In the meantime add 3/4 pint well salted broth to 12 oz. pearl barley. After 10 minutes of cooking over high heat, add 1 tablespoon butter to barley and mix, then place the covered pot in a hot oven in order for the barley to dry roast. Instead of the barley, rice may also be roasted, but the barley is much tastier.

Form the barley into a ring on a warmed, preferably round platter, place duck portions in the middle and pour sauce over the whole.

Young geese were prepared similarly in the Old Polish cuisine.

Mushroom Cutlets
(a Lent Dish)

Cook 2 oz. dried mushrooms until tender in a small amount of water. Cool, then grind in a meat grinder along with 2 white rolls that have been soaked in milk and squeezed out well. The rolls should weigh c. 5 oz. when dry. After adding 1 finely diced onion which as been fried in butter, 2 whole (small) eggs, salt and pepper to taste, knead the above ingredients by hand into a paste, then form small flat cutlets. Dip the cutlets in flour, egg and breadcrumbs, fry in butter or good salad oil and serve with potato sauce.

Potato sauce: This is an exquisitely tasting mild sauce which is highly valued in the Polish cuisine. It is served not only with mushroom cutlets, but also with boiled meat and with fried kiełbasa (Polish sausage).

Lightly brown 1 oz. flour in 1.5 oz. butter, at the same time adding a very finely diced medium onion to this. The onion should not brown, only simmer until tender. Thin down the roux gradually with 3/4 pint light broth. Add 4 grains of pimento (allspice) and a small piece of bay leaf. After 10 minutes of cooking over very low heat, put the sauce through a fine sieve. The sauce should be thin. Add 10 oz. very finely diced potatoes to the hot sauce. When the potatoes are tender but not overcooked, season sauce with the juice of 1/2 lemon, salt to taste and, if desired, add 1/2 teaspoon sugar.

Place the hot cutlets on a platter and pour very hot sauce over them. Just before serving, a tablespoon of very finely minced parsley sprigs may be added to the sauce.

Dried Mushrooms Just Like Fresh Mushrooms

Old Polish cuisine was very inventive and at the same time numerous garlands of fine dried mushrooms hung in pantries. Therefore, a way was found to prepare dried mushrooms that imitated the fresh variety. This dish was very popular on cold winter days. It is rather costly, but nevertheless worth trying out.

Wash briefly 8 oz. not too large dried mushroom caps. Pour cold milk over them so that the caps are covered. Leave overnight in the milk. Next day, add some water to the milk, cook the mushrooms over low heat until tender. Drain the mushrooms and slice thinly.

Melt 2 oz. butter in a frying pan. Lightly brown a finely diced medium onion in the butter. When onion begins to brown add 1/2 — 1 oz. flour and fry with the onion until the flour browns lightly as well. Thin down the flour and onion with the milk in which the mushrooms were cooked and with 1/4 pint sour cream. Now add the sliced mushrooms, salt and pepper to taste and simmer everything over low heat for 10 minutes, mixing constantly. Just before serving season the mushrooms with the juice of 1/2 lemon and with a tablespoon of finely minced parsley. Before serving check once more if the mushrooms are salted enough.

Mushrooms prepared in this manner may be a Lent dish or a very attractive addition to fried and roasted meats. They may also be used as a filling for omelets.

Old Polish Zrazy*
with Mushrooms and Cream

From tender beef (sirloin is best) cut small slices against the grain, pound lightly, sprinkle with freshly ground pepper and fry briefly in butter.

In 1 pint water cook 2 oz. dried mushrooms until tender. Slice the cooked mushrooms into strips, leaving the smaller caps whole. Arrange the meat slices in a saucepan, sprinkling them with the mushrooms, and cover with well-salted mushroom broth. Cover the saucepan tightly and simmer over low heat 20 minutes.

After this place 2 lbs. peeled potatoes not too thinly sliced in the saucepan. Cover the pan again, shake lightly and place over low heat once more. When potatoes are nearly tender, add 1/2 pint sour cream thoroughly mixed with a heaped teaspoon of wheat flour. Cook, covered, for another 10—12 minutes over very low heat.

---
* Beef slices.

Serve them in the saucepan in which they have been prepared (heat-proof casseroles are excellent for this purpose). This dish is recommended for a "man's" breakfast.

Roast Beef Roll with Mushrooms

This is a dish with a truly "Polish note", harmoniously uniting the flavours and aromas of meat and mushrooms. The

stuffing (stuffings or farces have been a part
of Polish cooking since the end of the
17th century) gives the roast an elegant
character, thus it may be served on more
festive occasions as a typically Polish
addition to the dinner or supper menu.

Pound a 2 lbs. piece of boneless rump
steak on a damp board to the thickness of
a small finger and sprinkle liberally with
the juice of 1 lemon.

Farce: Cook 2 oz. dried mushrooms in
2 cups of water until fully tender. 1 cup of
concentrated stock should remain after
cooking. If less remains, add boiling
water to make 1 cup.

When cool, grind the mushrooms with
2 oz. fat smoked bacon. Fry 2 finely diced
onions in 1 tablespoon butter. Combine
onions with the mushrooms and bacon,
adding 1 tablespoon breadcrumbs, 1 raw
egg, 1 tablespoon sour cream, 1 tablespoon
finely minced parsley sprigs and a considerable pinch of ground pepper. Mix everything and salt to taste.

Cover the meat evenly with the farce, roll tightly (tuck in the edges so that the farce does not run out during the roasting), and tie with a white cotton thread which has been scalded in boiling water. Sprinkle lightly with salt and brown on all sides in hot butter. Remove meat from oven-pan for a moment, so that finely chopped vegetables can be added: 1 carrot, 1 parsley root, 1/3 celeriac, 1 onion and, when in season, 1 kohlrabi. Place browned meat on the vegetables and pour mushroom stock over it. First stew the meat in a covered oven-pan over low heat for 30 minutes, then remove cover and roast in an oven. When too much sauce has evaporated, add some boiling water from time to time, whenever needed.

Remove thread from the meat. Carve meat not too thinly and pour the sauce, put through a sieve, over it.

Dry-roasted buckwheat kasha is served separately (with dill) along with green lettuce in summer and beets in winter.

Omelet Cake with Mushrooms

Polish cuisine adopted the art of making omelets during the reign of John III Sobieski. The queen, who was of French origin, was a great fan of light, delicate omelets that went well with the greatest variety of salted and sweetened, meat, mushroom, vegetable and fruit fillings. The queen's liking for the originally French omelets was well known. Thus, whenever the carriage with the royal pair (the king enjoyed travelling through the country) stopped for a brief rest at a nobleman's manor, the sound of eggs being beaten for omelets could be heard from the kitchen.

A well made omelet is, in spite of its utter simplicity, a dish worthy of a fastidious palate. And, as there was never a lack of eggs in Poland (they were one of the cheapest food products available), the culinary novelty propagated by the queen promptly found plenty of eager followers, especially since it was an inexpensive dish that could be prepared and served in minutes.

Omelets should be made in heavy cast-iron or aluminium frying pans. When made in thin tin frying pans they usually get burnt, which completely ruins their delicate flavour. Experienced housewives know this well, therefore we address this warning to beginners, just in case.

The omelet cake with mushrooms can be a main dish as well as a highly attractive side-dish.

Begin by preparing the mushroom filling.

Slice 1—1 1/2 lbs. fresh firm young mushrooms (boletus in summer are best, but may be substituted by champignons in winter) into thin strips and mince the stems finely. Simmer the mushrooms in butter with very finely minced onion (1 large onion or 2 small ones). When tender, add salt and pepper to taste and, if desired, flavour with 2—3 tablespoons thick sour cream. The mushroom filling should be thick!

Use two, or even three frying pans (depending on the number of people) of equal size for making the omelets, each consisting of 4 eggs. Beat the eggs briefly with a fork, salt moderately and, if desired, add one teaspoon very finely minced parsley. Pour egg mixture at once into the frying pan with hot, lightly browned butter. When omelets are done, remove them to a round platter, taking care not to fold them in the process. Place the hot filling on each omelet before placing another on top. Sprinkle the omelet on top, not covered with filling, with 1 tablespoon grated cheese (e.g. Emmenthaler or Parmesan) and pour melted butter over it liberally. Place the mushroom cake in a hot oven for several minutes, until it is lightly browned on top.

Green lettuce is served separately. The dressing is made from lemon, salad oil, a pinch of salt and a little sugar. (The salad bowl may also be rubbed with a clove of garlic before putting in the lettuce, which adds excellent flavour). If good dry red wine is served with this exquisite composition, the culinary success will be complete and fully deserved.

Scrambled Eggs with Mushrooms

Long before the appearance of omelets in the Polish cuisine, scrambled eggs were considered to be such a light dish that a grown man with a Polish appetite had no fewer than 10 scrambled eggs for breakfast or supper! And these were made with such additions as sausage or smoked bacon. Scrambled eggs with mushrooms were a particularly favoured Lent dish.

Slice 10 oz. young mushrooms (boletus or agaric) into thin strips, simmer in 1 — 2 oz. butter with 1 finely minced onion. Flavour the tender mushrooms with 3 tablespoons thick sour cream and when this begins to boil, beat in 4 — 5 eggs and add some finely minced parsley. If desired, the scrambled eggs may be sprinkled with the parsley when already done. Finely minced chives may also be sprinkled over them.

Make scrambled eggs over low heat, mixing constantly. When they reach the desired consistency, serve them in the frying pan in which they have been prepared. For breakfast bread and butter is served with them, for supper boiled potatoes and lettuce.

The above version of scrambled eggs can satisfy the appetites of 3 people, and, when served for supper, the moderate appetites of 4 people.

Agaric Mushrooms "from the Frying Pan"

Agaric mushrooms possess nothing but virtues and one great fault: they do not tolerate transportation when fresh. For this reason they seldom appear on city tables.

Their flavour, different and somewhat sharper than that of the boletus mushrooms, is equally exquisite. If it were not for this one fault, they could certainly compete with the boletus. They are tastiest when fried on a pan only in butter.

Having rinsed healthy, not too large mushrooms, drain them on a strainer and cut off the stems. Arrange mushrooms in a frying pan with very hot butter (do not skimp on the butter!), gill-side up. After several minutes of frying over high heat, turn the mushrooms over with a fork and fry the other side. In the beginning, when placed in the pan, they will let out juice. But when the butter regains its clarity and turns intensely orange, dust the mushrooms lightly with salt and serve at once, preferably in the pan in which they have been prepared.

Here is another version of agaric mushrooms from the frying pan that makes a good dinner dish provided there are enough mushrooms on hand. Fry the mushrooms as in the above recipe, then pour over them 1/2 cup sour cream. When the cream has cooked briefly, serve the mushrooms with dry-roasted buckwheat kasha (an excellent combination), or with potatoes.

Polish
Hospitality
and Social
Customs

Polish hospitality is generally

admired. Traditionally it goes back to old Slavic and pagan times. It is true that with the passing of time many old traditions have been forgotten, but hospitality is a virtue which has survived and is here to stay. It has been reborn with each generation in different forms, but has never changed in essence.

The history of Polish hospitality has passed through various times. The legendary Piast demonstrated this traditional hospitality when he warmly welcomed two travellers who had knocked in vain at the gate of the wealthy prince Popiel. To this day traditions of hospitality are alive in the Polish villages, which fact can be confirmed by the many tourists, particularly the young, whose tourist luggage often includes more eagerness to travel than ready cash.

A farmer's family that lives modestly not only astonishes us with the magnificence of a reception during a church holiday or wedding, but also with the dignified hospitality with which it receives the many invited guests. In older times wedding receptions were associated with ancient rites and traditional wedding dishes were served, such as the beautifully decorated wedding-cake. Today village weddings and other celebrations are less colourful as far as traditions are concerned. They have changed along with the forms of peasant hospitality, drawing nearer the ways of the city, which are not always the best models to follow. Even in past ages the Polish village often followed the customs of the gentry, which in numerous instances unfortunately set a bad example, often resulting in habitual alcoholism among the peasants. The nobleman produced vodka and beer and sold it to peasants on credit, thus drawing large profits for himself.

Little is said about village hospitality in Old Polish literature. It was well known and highly praised as a feature of the common folk in Poland.

The famous hospitality of the gentry and the magnates, on the other hand, was much written about, although it did not always have a good reputation. The Polish nobleman of any rank was a social person. He was courageous, fought with bravado, was an ardent hunter, a ladies' man who was very courteous towards the fair sex. He valued sumptuous good meals and strong drinks, usually indulging too much in both. He had a somewhat exaggerated notion of a nobleman's honour, which often resulted in a duel. His education varied, but most often he could speak sophisticated Latin fluently. He was an excellent companion, a faithful friend, at the same time being a dangerous foe, especially when his pride was hurt. He could combine religious fanaticism with patriotism, demanding for himself "gentry freedom" almost without limits, often bordering on factiousness. Thus elective kings, who reigned in Poland after the dying out of the Jagiellon dynasty, were at the mercy of the gentry, which constantly demanded greater privileges.

One could write plenty about the virtues and vices of the Polish nobleman of the 16th—18th centuries. They were combined in various ways and degrees into individualities where either virtues or vices prevailed, as is often the case today also. Virtues are more scarce today as well, and so they were and are greatly cherished.

Let us recall the prophetic words of the first Polish chronicler Gallus Anonymous, written nearly ten centuries ago. Gallus states that Poland "deserves to be extolled over others for the reason that, although surrounded by so many... Christian and pagan peoples and repeatedly invaded by all at the same time and each one separately, it has never been totally subjugated by any one".

Poland was called the bulwark of Christendom. Today it is difficult to tell what Europe's or Poland's fate would have been but for the courage of the knights who successfully held back the invasions of the hordes of Tartars and Turks, at the cost of much bloodshed. The young Polish king Ladislaus perished (1444) at Varna in a battle with the Turks in which much blood was shed. King John III Sobieski, at the head of his army, saved Vienna (1683), which was surrounded by the Turks. The Polish knights were also the bulwark of the Slavic peoples, holding back the German invasions into Slavic countries and suppressing the thirst for territorial conquest of the Teutonic Order, which had settled on Polish lands. A destructive avalanche of the Swedish army fell on Poland from the north. Thus we were constantly endangered from all sides. But even the greatest defeats, the tragic partitions and Hitler's occupation, did not succeed in erasing the Polish state or nation from the continuously changing political map of Europe.

The Polish nobleman was always ready to stand in the serried ranks of the Polish knights in order to defend the borders of his country. Sometimes whole generations spent more time at war than in the peaceful retreat of their homes. These circumstances were the decisive factors in the shaping of the customs of the nobleman-knight.

As a compensation for constantly coming face to face with death, the nobleman loved the frequently short life and its pleasures, which he fully indulged in during more peaceful times.

It is a known fact that the Polish nobleman disliked solitude. Manor-houses were scattered sparsely, roads were terrible, difficult for carriages and wagons to pass and easier for horseback riders. Shopping in the nearest town or a trip to the regional council or for any other business became a real expedition. Therefore, most manor-houses were self-sufficient worlds.

The appearance of a guest who was invited and dear to the host's heart, or of an uninvited guest, was a festive occasion for the whole household and added variety to the monotony of everyday life. Friendships were sealed with ease and quickly among gentry of equal rank, often after the first few glasses of drink, which were an introduction to the pleasures of the table, quickly prepared by the lady of the

house. Cooks appeared later and even then rather in the manors of the wealthy and the magnates. We have reason to suppose that these domestic dishes were more tasty than the ones made for a banquet, the latter being prepared more often with their showy appearance in mind. This is confirmed by Mikołaj Rej (1505—69), called the Father of Polish Literature, and many Old Polish epigrams by various authors. The atmosphere of a dinner-party with a small circle of guests was much more pleasant than that of the crowded noisy banquets of the magnates, which were given for masses of guests with the aim of winning over political supporters. An old proverb of the nobility says: "Seven a good meal, nine a bad deal." Another one adds: "Fight at a big gathering and eat at a small one."
There were banquets given by the magnates that were very elegant, but more about this later.
This modest menu described in a poem about the village manor even today evokes our approval and... appetite.

> *A good capon before festivities or carnival,*
> *Pork from a fatted, well-fed pig.*
> *I shall not refuse roast beef*
> *Or a mutton chop in autumn,*
> *Or veal with salad, or in addition*
> *To the salad — cucumbers.*

This praise comes from the poet Wespazjan Kochowski (1633—1700).
Another 17th century epigram enumerates the following "light and substantial dishes":

> *Toasts, mousses, kashas and soups; trifles;*
> *Goose, capon, roasts are dishes for eating;*
> *Scrambled eggs with bacon are a servant of these.*
> *Even cheese with bread is good, a quick dish under the sun.*

The local parish-priest was often invited to the table. The priest felt it to be his duty to bless in turn all the dishes brought in, instead of limiting himself only to making the sign of the cross before reaching for the spoon. This culinary devoutness is made fun of by the 17th century Polish poet, Olbrycht Karmanowski in the epigram entitled *Prayer to the Manorial Table*, which also mentions some of the popular dishes:

> *Thou, who has invited us to this table,*
> *Bless that, which is from the root and what is for the soup;*
> *Thou, who has created from nothing inaccessible heavens,*
> *Bless today this here loaf of bread.*
> *Saint Peter, having opened the unattainable stores,*
> *Bless the roast and this meat from the turnip.*
> *Dear Saint Helen with dear Saint Anne,*
> *Bless these sausages along with the pan...*

This is not poetry with higher aspirations for sure. But in Old Polish epigrams much of the lively, straightforward Old Polish language has been preserved so that when reading them, we feel as if we were transplanted to those distant but colourful times. The nobility adored epigrams and, when in merry company at the table, often read bawdy couplets which were sometimes even too outspoken. To this day the Polish temperament is widely known and deserves its reputation. The source of it is perhaps in the excessively substantial meals consisting of meats and fats and the equally excessive drink. No one at the nobleman's table remembered the warning of St. Jerome, who gave these admonitions in his *Letters*:

"Not the fires of Etna, nor Vulcan, nor Vesuvius, nor Olympus burn with such fire as the inner fire that consumes a youth intoxicated with wine and excited by food."

An agreement concluded in 1638 by the nobleman Drohojowski and the mayor of Bełżec, Nemorecki, tells us how youths on the brink of manhood were fed. The agreement dealt with the kind of food that the mayor was to give the nobleman's two sons who lived in lodgings at his house and the "pedagogue" who took care of the youths.

The document is long, so that we shall only give a summary:

dinner was to consist of four dishes, of these two were to
be of meat ("one capon for six persons, fair-sized pieces of
veal, a considerable piece of boiled beef that is not lean")
and two vegetable dishes ("carrots or turnips with fresh
meat, pickled or fresh cabbage, everything with fresh pork
fat"); as much cheese for dinner or supper "as they wish";
on Sundays and holidays a fifth dish (of meat): goose,
capon, veal or pork; on festive holidays "something else
besides this". For supper there should be three dishes: of
meat, vegetable ("with ample pieces of meat") and kasha
with meat, well flavoured. On Wednesdays, Fridays and
Saturdays for dinner "two portions of fish each, a vegetable
with butter, a vegetable with dairy products. For supper
fried or boiled eggs, cakes for six persons". For an afternoon
snack: "either bread with butter, or roasted sausage, or
fried bigos". Breakfast: "according to needs". Beer for
dinner, supper and between these "according to thirst".

The above is an authentic menu of a nobleman, not of
a magnate, since the sons of magnates did not attend
a school in Bełżec, but went abroad for education and
refinement. On such food the young Drohojowskis must
have been soon punished with "the fires of Etna and
Vesuvius".

Thus we know what was eaten in the average hospitable
nobleman's house. When a guest appeared the host greeted
him as warmly as if he had been exceptionally honoured,
even if the guest came unexpectedly, looking for a place to
spend the night and not finding an inn. And if the guests
were expected, the best treasures of the pantry and cellar
appeared on the table. Unfortunately, this Old Polish
hospitality was too often abused. A nobleman did not
set out on a journey without his servants, who had to be
made comfortable as well. There were many who took
advantage of this hospitality, constantly extending the
length of their stay, and leaving for new "visits" after the
host's pantry and cellar had been emptied. In spite of the
proverbial Polish hospitality, praised so highly by foreigners

visiting Poland, many bitter sayings went around about unwelcome guests. Let us quote the most popular of these: "An untimely guest is worse than a Tartar"; "Kill the man who invented keeping open house; better always to be a guest"; and the sharpest of all: "A guest and a fish stink on the third day."

There was also the custom of presenting gifts to the guests. It was enough that a guest admired a carpet, a piece of furniture, arms or even a horse and he received them at once as a gift. Thus hospitality had its worse side which deepened with time and the Old Polish proverb "A guest in the house, God in the house" slowly lost its original meaning.

The dining-room of a nobleman, usually in a wooden manor-house, was spacious and full of light, sometimes having as many as eight windows. There was little furniture in it. A table, benches and a usually large sideboard made up the essential furnishings. Rarely were there more costly pieces, such as the carved chairs of Gdańsk, which were usually made by the manor's cabinet-maker. In spite of the modest furnishings, the interior of the house did not give the impression of being poor. On the contrary, the table, benches, sideboard, walls and — particularly on special occasions — the floor, were covered with numerous, often very costly carpets, either from conquests or purchased from Armenian merchants. These carpets, tapestries and ornamented painted fabrics which often covered the walls, gave an elegant and luxurious appearance even to a manor-house of average wealth. The walls were also decorated with arms and family portraits. Silver and gold-plated dishes, pitchers and goblets and later costly glass and porcelain were placed on the sideboard. The main decoration, however, was the carpets, which noblemen collected with a particular fondness.

In winter a fire burnt in the dining-room, sometimes the fireplace being decorated with marble and the host's coat-of-arms. A nobleman felt that "the stove gave only heat and was deaf and dumb; a fireplace gave both heat and light and talked with a person".

Before sitting down to the table, the tapestry runner was covered with a snow-white tablecloth on which plates and dishes with food were placed.

This was how many small manor-houses of average wealth looked. In richer manor-houses, in castles and palaces, priceless treasures that astounded foreigners were collected from generation to generation. To this must be added the treasures of monasteries and churches, and the splendid homes of the burghers.

During the countless wars that ravaged Poland, this whole wealth was lost by fire and plunder. If not for the enormous losses over the centuries, we could compete with the wealthiest countries of Europe, which were treated more kindly by history.

As early as 1596 Paulo Mucante, secretary and Master of Ceremonies of the papal legate, Enrico Cardinal Gaetano, noted in his journal that the Cracow market square was larger than the famous Italian market squares, that one "can buy anything here from glass to lemons", all kinds of meat of the highest grade, game and poultry, that the stalls are very clean and prices are "extremely low", that in the shops of Cracow merchants there are the highest luxury items from all of Europe. Finally, he states with true admiration:

"I cannot believe that there could be another city as abundantly supplied with everything as Cracow and it is just to quote the old saying that if Rome did not exist, Cracow would be Rome."

It is interesting to note these views of a foreigner who knew many European cities and was seen at many courts, and to reflect that they were noted down in the year when the decision to transfer the capital from Cracow to Warsaw was taken, that is when the importance and splendour of the city began to wane slowly.

Paulo Mucante had no reason to bestow compliments,

especially since the "delicate" mission of his master, Cardinal Gaetano, which aimed at drawing Poland into the war with the Turks, failed. He noted down things as they were, having seen them with his own eyes.

From many old accounts, epigrams and journals we learn how ruinous some visits were for the host. For example, the author of the famous memoirs, Jan Chryzostom Pasek (1636—1701), happened to be host in his village manor to the Minsk voivode, Zawisza. Pasek's fortune was far from that of a magnate, he even had serious financial problems. Yet he received the guest admirably, beyond his modest means. The voivode recalls this visit in the following words:

"In Cisów I was waited on by Master Pasek, a man of disgraceful amiability. For three days we knew not night from day; we caroused and made merry. He had plenty of ladies at his house, who were truly beautiful. He presented me with a beautiful brass casket made in Kielce, along with a dressing-table of the same make, a polished case et cetera et cetera."

It may be supposed that also magnates and kings presented gifts to their guests, especially to illustrious foreigners, envoys and papal nuncios. These gifts were unbelievably costly and exquisite.

Our ancestors were said not to be masters of elegant conversation. However, they could tell very good, absorbing and colourful tales. The main subjects of such story-telling at the table were war adventures, hunting reminiscences and genealogical commentaries concerning the guest's and host's coats-of-arms. Since both the listeners and the narrators drank heartily, alcohol worked on the imagination, stretching true facts into almost fantastic tales. This did not bother anyone as long as the tale was interesting.

With time, however, our ancestors learnt the art of witty conversation quite well, often flavouring it with a sharp humour. Guillaume de Beauplan, who was in Poland during the reign of Sigismund III Vasa (1587—1632) and of his son Ladislaus IV (1632—48), was fascinated by the social virtues of Poles, stating that in this respect they equalled the French. He also praised the Polish cuisine and Polish fish dishes in particular. He wrote down in his journal that in preparing fish Poles are "masters and surpass other nations". Such a compliment, coming from a Frenchman, was greatly valued.

Conversation blossoms best at a well-laid table, in well chosen and not too numerous company since it is the common fruit of intellectual, social and culinary culture.

Even the long and florid orations, which were favoured by Poles of old and delivered at any occasion, more and more frequently contained a portion of very good jokes.

For example, during the wedding-feast of the grand chancellor of the crown Jan Wielopolski and the sister of King John III Sobieski's wife, Louise Marianne d'Arquien in 1678, Voivode Jabłonowski, giving the bride away to the groom, is said to have delivered a long oration expatiating on the symbolic meaning of her coat-of-arms, in which the shield was ornamented by three hammers, three stags and three lilies. He underlined that the bride "comes from sixteen French kings".

Hetman Sieniawski answered in the name of the bridegroom with one terse sentence:

"I do not comment on the origin of coats-of-arms, but merely state that the horse of the bridegroom's coat-of-arms will know how to graze on these lilies."

One can imagine the outburst of laughter of the good company and the jovial mood with which guests sat down to the exquisitely laid tables.

It is not in vain that in old Poland it was said that "a good joke is worth a *tynf**".

The feasts of the magnates, prepared for the less important gentry, were different — crowded and noisy. In spite of the numerous courses, the best dishes were served only at

---

* *Tynf* or *tymf*: a silver coin issued in 1663—67.

the main table. The quantity of dishes resulted in their careless preparation. Drinking took place without any limits and countless toasts were raised, the first one being for the king or the wealthy host. Such feasts often came to a sad end, leaving the dining-room in a deplorable state. If women took part in it, they usually left the table when the repast began to change into a chaotic drinking bout; it was then that quarrels took place, sometimes ending in bloodshed, since swords were not put away when guests sat down to eat.

> *After yesterday's banquet I leave the room,*
> *Plenty of blood, glass, filth on all sides;*
> *A priest is led to one man, a surgeon to another,*
> *Some are making up their quarrel, others starting*
> *a fight...*

These are the words of an eye-witness and participant of such feasts, the poet Wacław Potocki (1621—96).

Women, of course, always sat down to the table whenever pleasant or distinguished guests were received and when less numerous company suited them, and observed good banqueting manners. During the toast in their honour, the ladies drank a few drops of wine, which meant that the toast, usually full of compliments, was favourably received. In a closed family circle the ladies were not always so restrained. Women also took part in the magnificent banquets of the magnates and kings. Without the participation of women, in particular young and beautiful ones, the dinner was less attractive. This is confirmed by Wespazjan Kochowski in one of his epigrams:

> *Salt, wine and good will go to make up a feast.*
> *There's a fourth ingredient: one woman at least.*

And when the meal often ended with music and dance:

> *Young ladies in pairs come in and bow*
> *And lead the dance, holding hands,*
> *Until they draw out the merry youths from the table:*
> *Who dance in an orderly fashion in a circle.*

Wedding feasts were the grandest of family celebrations.

The men and women of the two newly-joined families and guests appeared in their finest garments. With the Polish nobleman's attire sparkling with precious stones and the lively colours of costly fabrics, the sight of the wedding procession must have been fascinating.

While speaking of weddings, let us say a few words about two soups which were feared by youths in love. A young man, when coming to ask for the hand of his chosen lady, even if he was not accepted by the lady and her parents, was first treated to a dinner. A refusal was not necessarily given in words. When the *czarna polewka* (black soup made with blood) was served, it meant that the wooer was refused. A similar role was played by thick *grochówka* (pea soup) with pig-tails. Lying in the soup the tails meant refusal, and gaily upright consent. After being served the "refusal soup", the unfortunate wooer usually took his leave.

Towards the end of the 16th century the older light ale was replaced by spirits widely distilled at home. There were supposedly as many as 200 various types of Polish alcoholic beverages. It was not only a "plebeian drink". It was also drunk by magnates, the Elector of Saxony and the Polish King Augustus II the Strong (1697—1706). Even ladies kept variously flavoured alcoholic beverages in the medicine-cabinet within reach, trying out their effectiveness behind the men's backs.

Towards the end of the 18th century, after the fashion for home-made alcoholic beverages, came the fashion for wine. Plenty of it had been drunk much earlier, but only then did it take first place. It was imported from Italy, France, Spain, Crete and Hungary. Sometimes great fortunes were drowned in drink. Abstinence was not practised in other European countries either. For example, in the 18th century in England the consumption of alcohol (gin) was much greater than in Poland. The latest studies also tell us that the widespread opinion about the hard drinking habits of peasants and poorer folk in older Poland is rather exaggerated. There were those who called for temperance, but they were hardly heeded.

> *God made man from clay, so history says:*
> *Does he not soak through on his drinking days?*

wondered a poet concerned with the drinking habits of the gentry.

During the reign of the Saxon kings the royal court set the worst example.

The castellan Borejko has come down to us as an example of the deplorable customs of the Saxon era. The castellan was a tragicomic caricature of the old virtues of the gentry: hospitality, generosity and piety. Borejko willingly drank with the clergy. Therefore, he often turned to nearby monasteries to ask for two monks to be sent "for company". Naturally "the bravest ones" were sent. Having gathered enormous quantities of drinks and food in the rooms, he locked the chambers, announcing that from that moment on they were a monastery to which the entrance of outsiders was forbidden. In the morning the bell was rung for mass, then for meals and finally, when alcohol had felled everyone to the ground, for silentium. Only the priest, who was to conduct mass the next morning, drank until 11 o'clock at night. The repast began immediately after morning mass, with breakfast. The breviary, which was obligatory for the clergy, was not forgotten and the devout Borejko took part in it himself.

This conduct lasted for 3 do 5 days, after which the clerics left for their monasteries with gifts from the host.

During Saxon times even moderate asceticism was rarely practised in monasteries. What went on behind the walls of the mendicant orders is colourfully described in the mock-heroic poem entitled *Monachomachia* written in 1778 by one who should know, since he was himself the bishop of Warmia and at the same time one of the greatest poets of the Polish Enlightenment, Ignacy Krasicki (1735—1801).

There were many boon companions wearing a monk's habit. The most widely known in this field, however, were the Bernardine mendicant friars, who distinguished themselves by a "supernatural" endurance in drinking.

Until the end of the 17th century the Polish royal court was considered to be one of the most elegant courts in Europe. Guests were received with splendour, pomp and ceremony. We shall describe briefly how in 1596 King Sigismund III received the papal legate Gaetano and the accompanying nuncio. Since the king was in mourning after the death of his first wife, the reception was not only characterized by splendour but also by gravity. Three separate tables were laid for the king, the cardinal and the nuncio. The king's table and the walls of the hall were covered with black cloth. The plates and bread-basket on the king's table were of pure gold. The entrance of the king and the guests was unusually ceremonious. The table was blessed not only by the chaplain, but by the cardinal. "Richly embroidered towels were spread out before these three persons, pitchers of rock crystal were brought in; after endless bows, water was given to the king, the cardinal and the nuncio. Separate platters were brought in for each and each platter was followed by bows and courtesies without end: by the one who brought in the platters, the one who carved and served the meat, that is: first the royal chef to the carver with bows, he in turn to the royal carver, who dipped a piece of bread in the dish, put it to his tongue and threw it into a large silver basket that stood nearby. The king and the cardinal had to wait a long time because of these rites, before they could begin eating... As soon as the king sat down, the prelates and noblemen sat down too and began to eat. Whenever the king drank, the nuncio rose, took off his cap and stood; the cardinal wanted to rise, but the king did not allow it."

The banquet was a little too stiff for Polish temperaments, but perfectly suited to the occasion, in view of the court mourning and guests representing the highest ranks of the church hierarchy.

In 1646, when Princess Marie Louise de Gonzague-Nevers came to Poland to marry the son of Sigismund III Vasa, King Ladislaus IV, she was greeted just as magnificently. The welcome (the king awaited his bride in Warsaw) took place in Gdańsk. During the reception the table was laid with costly plates, covered with four tablecloths and each course (consisting of many dishes) was served on a different one. The first tablecloth was white, the second one was of crimson satin, the third of gold, silver and silk threads embroidered with flowers, the last one was white. The wedding feast itself, at the Warsaw castle, was even more magnificent.

Let us say a few words about the dinner set. Already during the feast given by Boleslaus the Brave the table was laden with silver and gold dishes. The luxurious dinner sets of Polish tables had long-standing traditions in the homes of the wealthiest. The poorer folk ate on pewter plates, the poorest on wooden plates which before long were replaced by pewter and clay, often beautifully painted and glazed.

Finally, there was also faience, porcelain and table glass. These were unusually costly dishes imported from Italy, sometimes of great artistic value and more expensive than silver dishes. However, in the first half of the 18th century faience became commonplace and less expensive, while on tables there appeared Saxon, Viennese, Sèvres and — the most expensive — Chinese and Japanese porcelain. Polish dinner services were not only not inferior to those from other countries, but also surpassed them in splendour. The Poles even developed a certain distinctive style in this field. A feature of the Polish table, even that of a nobleman, was the so-called "service". According to one of the chroniclers of Old Polish culture, this was a glass, silver or wooden tray with a silver surround. On it there were silver- or gold-plated miniature summer-houses, gardens, baskets with fruits, etc. The whole was covered with a dome adorned with the Polish eagle with its wings spread out, or with an allegorical figure. There were also smaller and more modest "services" for everyday use, which were called *menaziki*.

Such an ingenious "service" which decorated the table during "the last Old Polish banquet" is described by Adam Mickiewicz in the 12th volume of *Pan Tadeusz*:

> *Meanwhile the guests sat waiting, as they gazed*
> *At the great centrepiece and were amazed*
> *At its fine workmanship and metal wrought.*
> *Radziwiłł, called the Orphan, it was thought,*
> *Had had it made in Venice by command*
> *With Polish decorations, which he planned.*
> *It had been taken in the Swedish wars,*
> *And found its way back here by some strange course.*
> *Today it had been brought out from the hoard,*
> *And like a cart-wheel occupied the board.*
> *Whipped cream and icing sugar white as snow*
> *Covered the centrepiece, which seemed to show*
> *A winter landscape. In the midst you see*
> *A darkling forest of confectionery,*
> *And village houses round about it gleam*
> *With frosty covering of sugar cream,*
> *And little china figures decorate*
> *In Polish dress the edges of the plate...* *

Not everyone could afford even the simplest *menazik*, which was, after all, a costly object of luxury. But this does not mean that the table of smaller manors was laid in any careless fashion. It was decorated with flowers which were often wild. These were not tall bouquets but a not too wide band of multi-coloured petals running along the centre of the table. These were often artistic ornaments. The

* Cf. pp. 258—259.

daughters of the host and young girls were skilled in this, as they were usually excellent embroidresses, possessing considerable experience in the art of decoration.

Much can be written about Old Polish spoons. They were often real wonders of the goldsmith's art, particularly the silver and gold-plated spoons. On the handles humorous sayings were engraved and on the outer part of the bowl the owner's coat-of-arms. Forks appeared on Polish tables earlier than in France and in the 17th century they were already widely used. These were also beautifully decorated. For example, we know that the poet Wacław Potocki quoted earlier bought a knife and fork for himself in Cracow, inlaid with ivory and for his wife a set decorated with coral.

Towards the end of the 16th century, at the more elegant banquets, napkins were placed by the plates. In the 17th century expensive damask napkins from Cologne and the Netherlands were used in Poland.

Such delicacies as nuts, raisins and figs also became popular. In the 18th century they were imported in great quantities from the East, mainly from Turkey. There are oriental influences in some of the Polish sweet cakes and in such drinks as rose water, almond milk and refreshing lemonades. Ignacy Krasicki definitely preferred Old Polish cakes. When he tasted some Turkish cakes brought by his nephew from Turkey, he wrote in one of the letters: "He brought me cakes from a Grand Turk, but if the Grand Turk is worth as much as these cakes, then — dear sir — the Grand Turk is not worth much."

However, the journey from Turkey to the bishop's residence took several weeks in those times, the cakes were probably stale, and Krasicki was a great gourmet.

The reign of Augustus II (1697—1706; 1709—33) and Augustus III (1733—63) of Saxony was tragic in its disorganization of the state and the decline of the great prestige that Poland had among the leading European countries until then. Those times probably form the most

lamentable chapters in Polish history. The Polish cuisine had
seen better times as well. The widespread drinking of those
days was not favourable to the true moderation of a gourmet
cuisine.

However, during that period a few valuable novelties must
be noted, among them potatoes, coffee, tea and chocolate.
These were not absolute novelties, making their first appearance on Polish tables, but they now became widely
popular.

Potatoes appeared in Poland for the first time during the
reign of John III Sobieski, following his famous victory
over the Turks beleaguering Vienna. The king sent some
potato tubers (which were grown as a rarity in the Viennese
gardens of the emperor), recommending that they be
planted in his residence in Wilanów. The potatoes took
to the fertile Polish soil at once. When they were served
to guests invited by the king, they did not evoke enthusiasm
among the banqueters, who were used to cereals. However,
they did gain popularity and the son-in-law of the
royal gardener began to grow them on a wider scale,
making good profits on them as he had the Warsaw
magnates as clients, who paid well for a fashionable
vegetable. Potatoes became acclimatized in Poland during
the reign of Augustus III. The monarch invited Germans
to settle on Polish royal estates who planted potatoes, and
popularized them among Polish peasants. There was some
resistance to this. Some priests tried to persuade the peasants
that potatoes were bad for their health, even though
they themselves ate them with appetite. They were afraid
that if potato flour was added to wheat flour, wafers made
from such a mixture would not be suitable for liturgical
purposes and their use would have been sacrilege. However,
the priests' anxieties proved to be very exaggerated. Thus,
potatoes were brought into Polish kitchens "from above"
during the reign of John III and "from below" during
the reign of his successors, so that at the end of the reign
of Augustus III potatoes were known everywhere in Poland,

Lithuania and Ruthenia. Let us add that wafers were never made from potato flour in Poland, but during the reign of Stanislaus Augustus (1764—95) vodka was already distilled from potatoes.

When a sack of potatoes was sent to the camp at Berdyczów as an original gift for Kazimierz Pułaski (1747—79), famed both in Poland and America, the cook did not know at first what to do with them. But his intuition gave him the perfect solution: he cooked the peeled potatoes in salted water, seasoned them highly and served them with scrambled eggs, "and everyone present praised this new dish highly".

Potatoes were also prepared in villages, often with ingenuity and in unusually tasty ways. One of these methods, especially favoured by shepherds who spent the whole day far away from their village, is very popular to this day, particularly among young hikers and campers.

Potatoes Shepherd Style

For this recipe a cast-iron enamelled deep pot is needed. Thin strips of pork fat are placed on the bottom of the pot, followed by layers of sliced raw potatoes, onions and pork fat or smoked fat bacon. Each layer is sprinkled with salt and pepper. The top layer consists of potatoes, which are covered with 2—3 leaves of cabbage. The opening of the pot is sealed tightly with a circle of turf placed on the cabbage leaves. In the meantime a fire is lit and when it begins to die out, the glowing embers are placed around the pot and the fire is rekindled slightly. After about 40—45 minutes the potatoes are ready. After carefully removing the turf and cabbage leaves, the company eats this dish with spoons, sitting around the pot.

This dish, called *prażonka* in some areas, can be improved with 1—2 layers of thinly sliced sausage. It can also be eaten with pickles.

During the time when the great Johann Sebastian Bach, after many efforts nominated "court composer to the King of Poland and Elector of Saxony" in 1736 by Augustus III, was writing his famous *Kaffee-Kantate* (coffee cantata), this beverage was also known and valued in Poland, although only in higher circles. The victory of King John III Sobieski over the Turks at Vienna in 1683 was responsible for this. The brave Pole Kulczycki received great supplies of coffee taken from the Turkish camp as his booty and soon opened the first café in Vienna. However, Poles did not take a liking to coffee at once. Thirteen years before the Vienna victory, the poet Andrzej Morsztyn (1620—93) still wrote about coffee without enthusiasm:

> *In Malta, I remember, we tasted coffee,*
> *A drink for pashas, Murad, Mustafa*
> *And all the rest of Turks, but such a hideous*
> *Drink, like an ugly poison and venom*
> *Which does not whet any appetite,*
> *Let it not contaminate Christian mouths...*

In 1724 one of the courtiers of Augustus II opened the first café in Warsaw and in 1759 the Polish Jesuit Krusiński published a treaty under the scholarly title *Pragmatographia de Legitimo Usu of Turkish Ambrosias, That Is a Description of the Proper Way of Using Turkish Coffee*. Coffee, at first very expensive, quickly became cheaper and widely popular. Women in particular adored it. The good priest Kitowicz writes with slight disapproval: "If each day ten homes (as is easy in cities) were visited by one lady fond of coffee, she would not refuse a cup in any of them, wherever it was proposed to her; and it was the custom to offer this drink to guests.".

Coffee contributed greatly to the fight against alcoholic drink. "In the morning it was drunk with cream, during Lent with boiling water or milk, after dinner it was drunk black or with cream, whichever way was preferred, and

any man who drank it after dinner refrained from drinking
alcohol for two hours, he was under the protection of the
ladies, he belonged to their society. At their request and
with the excuse that it was bad for his health, he was
released absolutely from the obligation to drink," relates
the knowledgeable chronicler of those times, Łukasz
Gołębiowski.
With typical Polish generosity Polish women used the
best brands freely. They roasted the coffee at home,
directly before brewing it. It is no wonder that foreigners
went into raptures over "Polish coffee", and Adam Mickiewicz wrote about Old Polish coffee in *Pan Tadeusz* in the
following way:

> *There is no coffee like the Polish kind;*
> *In all well-ordered households you will find*
> *A special coffee-maker — 'tis her charge*
> *To purchase from the river-trader's barge*
> *Or from the city store the finest beans,*
> *And to prepare it she has secret means,*
> *As black as coal, as amber clearly glowing,*
> *As mocha fragrant, thick as honey flowing.* *

Tea was less popular in the older Polish cuisine than
coffee. In the beginning it was used as an effective
medicine in disorders of the stomach. Later it was
considered to be an elegant beverage, served in fashionable
salons more from snobbery than from conviction. It gained
the highest popularity in the Polish lands taken over by
Russia during the partitions. It was drunk in various ways:
the pure brew, with cream, with lemon, with raspberry
or cherry juice and with red wine.
Before tea was accepted, it was described with disrespect
or even with hostility. In 1703 Tomasz Ormiński,
professor at the Zamość Academy, objectively recognized
the following features in it:
"What do leaves of Thee do? Remove sleep without harm,
therefore merchants who must write a lot at night drink

* *Cf. p. 42*

Thee; it helps much for the stomach, I used this herb
myself a little, but I favour coffee more."
A stubborn, not to say fanatical enemy of tea was the
priest Jan Krzysztof Kluk, who wrote in his *Dictionary of
Plants*, published by himself in 1786—88:
"If China sent us all her poisons, she could not harm us as
much as with her tea." The learned priest exaggerated
greatly, but even though he freely expressed his disapproval,
he could not hold back the growing popularity of tea in
18th century Poland.
A cup of hot, fragrant chocolate for breakfast, drunk right
after waking up in bed, was a beverage of the lords,
fashionable during the reigns of Saxon kings and the last
Polish king, Stanislaus Augustus. But the majority preferred
coffee, so that the popularity of chocolate did not last long
and it was soon after degraded to the ranks of a beverage served to children for their afternoon snack.
Jerzy Ossoliński (1595—1650), the great chancellor of the
Crown, eminent diplomat and politician of wide vision,
the closest adviser to King Ladislaus IV — also has his
name written down on the pages of Polish culinary history.
He called on the magnates and rich nobility to practise
moderation in their great expenditure on expensive delicacies
imported from abroad, because what the country produced
itself was enough to add splendour to the most elegant
feast. Polish gold flowed abroad in great quantities, in
return for spices, wines, sugar, lemons and the like.
In order to convince everyone that he was right, he gave
a banquet made up of only Polish products, inviting
"a considerable number of noblemen" and all the foreign
envoys present in Warsaw at the time. The banquet was
a success in every way and the host "treated everyone to
such things that there was not only contentment but also
admiration on the part of the guests".
Instead of wine, cherry juice was added to sauces, instead
of almonds, there were various domestic nuts. Raisins were
substituted by dried cherries and other fruit candied not

in the very expensive sugar, but in honey. The food was soured not with lemons, but with tart apples; instead of pepper and ginger, horseradish and mustard were used. Dried and fresh mushrooms replaced olives and capers. Even vinegar, produced from wine in noblemen's homes, was made from honey.

The chronicler assures us that thirst was quenched with great contentment with Polish drinks: "There were various beers from various places, of excellent quality, mellow and delicious, any kind one wished to please his palate: from Warka, Łowicz, Końska Wola, Drzewice, Brzeziny, Odrzywola and Gielnia; meads that were also excellent... from Sandomierz country — white and red wine."

Ossoliński's Polish banquet was a social event widely commented on but treated as an eccentric joke. Foreign influences were in any case adapted to typically Polish tastes. Contrary to appearances, the majority of the gentry were rather conservative in culinary matters, especially in the everyday food served at home.

After the Polish-Lithuanian union of 1569 many excellent Lithuanian dishes that appealed to Polish tastes came to the Polish tables. Lithuanians, on the other hand, adopted many Polish dishes. During the reign of Sigismund the Old Italian cuisine was mainly popular at the royal court and also at magnate manors. The urban patricians, largely of foreign, especially German origin, contributed to the variety of Polish culinary recipes. Oriental influences became obvious during the reign of John III Sobieski. During the reign of the Saxon Kings Augustus II and Augustus III, potatoes were accepted permanently in Polish cooking. The last Polish king, Stanislaus Augustus Poniatowski, favoured French cooking, but did not shun genuinely Polish dishes. During the partitions, on the lands seized by the various powers, the influence of Russian and Austrian cuisines became marked. But Prussian cuisine, not being very popular in Europe, definitely did not make a favourable impression on Poles.

However, these numerous culinary influences did not disturb the essence of the Old Polish cuisine, which has retained its distinct national character till the present.

The well-paid foreign cooks who continuously came to Poland were enthusiastic propagators of culinary novelties.

The cuisine of the magnates was the first to lose its national character, easily falling under foreign influence and snobbery. The fantastic fortunes of many Polish magnates allowed for practically boundless luxuries and the fulfilment of every whim and fancy.

It was as late as 1682 that the first truly Polish cookbook appeared: *Compendium Ferculorum or a Collection of Dishes — by Stanisław Czerniecki, Culinary Chef... Written ad Usum Publicum*. This little work, today one of the rarest bibliophilic items, is a written monument of the magnificent Old Polish cuisine. Naturally, it contains not only Polish recipes. But the Polish recipes appear first and the author writes in his preface: "It need not cause distress that I begin my very first book with Polish dishes... It appeared to me that you should first try Old Polish dishes and if you do not find contentment in them, I then refer you to other more special ones."

Compendium Ferculorum was very popular until the 19th century. Adam Mickiewicz used it when recreating the picture of the last Old Polish feast in the 12th chapter of *Pan Tadeusz*.

The great poet made use not only of Czerniecki's work, but also *The Perfect Cook* by Wojciech Wielądko, many times reprinted (one such reprinting was in 1812).

However, the works of Czerniecki and Wielądko were not the first cookbooks written in Polish. The first one appeared as early as the 16th century, but was read and re-read so much that not one copy has survived until today.

The list of Polish cookbooks published until the end of the 10th century does not contain too many items. Probably the written word was often replaced by a carefully cultivated tradition that was passed on from generation to generation.

The Days of
King
Stanislaus
Poniatowski

Following the dark period of

the "Saxon night", the Polish Enlightenment made efforts to revive the great European traditions of the Polish Renaissance.

In the 16th century Poland was still an important power, and even though it was never free of enemies, Polish might evoked their respect. This was the golden age of Polish culture, which spread to other lands. Cracow University had many eminent European scholars among its staff.

These were the times of Nicolaus Copernicus (1473—1543), whose work entitled *De Revolutionibus Orbium Coelestium* created a scientific revolution. Then there were Jan Kochanowski (1530—84), creator of a poetic language of captivating beauty, Andrzej Frycz Modrzewski (1503—72) whose work *Commentariorum de Republica Emendanda* was widely read and commented on in all of Europe, the poet Klemens Janicki (1516—42), son of a Polish peasant, who had a poet's laurels bestowed on him in Padua, and many other outstanding scholars and artists.

The political and cultural situation of Poland looked completely different at the time when the last Polish king, Stanislaus Augustus Poniatowski, came to the throne in 1764. He found the country in a state of utter chaos and anarchy, brought about by the great magnate families who fought among themselves and — to achieve greater influence — were often in the service of foreign powers hostile to Poland. Even the lesser gentry, engaged in politics and confused by the magnate feuds, wishing to keep all its privileges at the cost of the peasants and townsfolk, became a dangerous unenlightened element, hard to control. This was the heritage that Stanislaus Augustus took on when he came to the throne at the wish of the Empress Catherine II, to be dethroned also at her will in 1795.

In such a situation it was difficult to reign and impossible to rule. And yet Stanislaus Augustus Poniatowski, although himself unstable and surrounded by enemies, attempted to do this.

The Constitution, which was passed by the Four-Year Seym and sworn in by the king on 3 May 1791, was the first government act of its kind in Europe and created a chance for far-reaching progressive reforms. Unfortunately, it was annulled as early as the following year by the Targowica Confederation of the magnates, supported by the intervening Russian army. The National Education Commission was active for a longer period and was the first central educational authority, a prototype of a ministry of education. Called into being at the initiative of the king, it marked an important turning-point in Polish education, making it democratic and secular and raising its standards. Unfortunately, it ceased to exist on the eve of the last partition of Poland in 1795.

There is no doubt that in different political conditions the Polish Enlightenment, whose leading representatives were grouped around the king, could have made Poland one of the most progressive countries of the Europe of those days. But it was too late to carry out the reforms which had been passed. However, a healthy seed of progressive thought had been planted, to sprout at a much later date. Stanisław Staszic (1755—1826), the leading representative of radical reforms, said these words after the third partition of Poland in 1795:

"Even a great nation can fall, but only a despicable nation can deteriorate." Indeed, Poland was spreading its wings during the days of Stanislaus Augustus until they were treacherously clipped.

In only a few lines we have made a sketch of the background against which we will try to show the person of Stanislaus Augustus as a patron of the sciences and fine arts, leaving the evaluation of his political activity to historians and history. Although it may sound ironic, the last Polish king was one of the most enlightened although at the same time one of the most powerless rulers of those days, and not only a refined aesthete and sybarite. He was the latter, no doubt, but not exclusively.

The Thursday Dinners

Wishing to establish more direct, unofficial contacts with scholars and artists, Stanislaus Augustus invited them to dinner on Thursdays. Not more than 10—12 persons took part at one time, which created an intimate atmosphere, especially since among the guests there were also persons who only listened to the conversation without taking an active part in it.

This was a novelty much commented on in Poland, even though these kinds of "intellectual dinners" already had splendid traditions in Europe. They were called "Thursday dinners", "scholastic dinners", "rational dinners", and "literary dinners".

These dinners took place, not always regularly, in the years 1771—81, at the Warsaw castle, or at the lovely Łazienki palace, which had been built as the summer residence of the king.

Aside from these Thursday dinners, to which literary men and scholars were invited by the king, there were also the less well-known Wednesday dinners, during which painters and architects sat at the table. Apparently the king felt that it was better to invite representatives of such varied arts separately, if only because of the subjects discussed. Even though Stanislaus Augustus spoke several languages fluently, including French — which was fashionable in higher circles then — only Polish was spoken at the table. The king had a good sense of humour and appreciated jokes. The king's favourite, the poet-chamberlain Tomasz Kajetan Węgierski (1756—87), knew this very well when he wrote the well-known epigram poking fun at guests who were more distinguished than him, and containing a clever compliment to the host:

> *And the learned dinners? A name that is odd,*
> *For half are silent and the other half nod.*
> *The king himself must cover the whole cost,*
> *Provide humour, wit, and wine and the roast.*

In the castle the smaller room "for the Thursday dinners" was decorated with portraits of representatives of Polish culture particularly esteemed and liked by the king. There were twenty portraits, all of them by Louis Marteau, the court painter of Augustus III and Stanislaus Augustus, of French origin, who came to Warsaw in 1743 and stayed there till his death.

Marcello Bacciarelli (1731—1818) was another court painter highly esteemed in Europe. He was the author of the well-known portrait of Stanislaus Augustus in his coronation robes. He also painted a cycle of portraits of 22 Polish kings at the order of the king, which were hung in the Marble Room of the Warsaw castle, and was the author of many canvases on historical subjects, plafonds etc. As "director of the royal painting workshop", Bacciarelli educated a whole school of Polish painters.

In the years 1767—80 the Italian painter Bernardo Bellotto called Canaletto, famous throughout Europe, stayed in Warsaw on the invitation of the king. His masterly pictures of the Warsaw of King Stanislaus' era were of great service during the reconstruction of the historic districts, palaces and churches of the capital destroyed by the Nazis.

We mention these outstanding painters not only because they took part in the Wednesday dinners, but above all because their activity had a stimulating effect on the development of Polish painting.

But let us return to the Warsaw castle and to its dining-room. The king sat at a round table with his guests, which was to show that all seats were of equal rank.

The dishes were too simple for the magnates' tastes of those days, but they were prepared and served with elegance. They were the creations of Paweł Tremo, who in Warsaw was considered to be "the first culinary chef of Europe".

The king was demanding, but he was a gourmet who valued moderation in food. The French cuisine suited him best. He had appreciated its attractiveness and lightness already in his youth during his stay in Paris, when he often visited the salon of Mme Geoffrin, which was well known among the intellectuals. The master-cook Tremo was able to combine the virtues of French cooking with the good traditions of Old Polish cooking, thus pleasing the culinary taste of the king.

Unfortunately we know only a few of the dishes served during the Thursday and Wednesday dinners. Among other items there were the traditional Polish soup — borsch with *uszka* — various cold meats served as hors d'oeuvres, patties and spicy marinades, various roasts, led by the king's favourite — roast mutton — which was served on a large silver platter by a courtier calling out "mutton". Fish and vegetables were also served. We have no information, however, about the Thursday desserts. It could be that Stanislaus Augustus did not care for sweets, although we know that right after waking up he drank a cup of hot chocolate or concentrated bouillon in bed.

Therefore the list is not complete, even if we add to it one of the famous and admired creations of Tremo: "hazel grouse unusually larded". This "unusual" character probably meant that it was larded not with the commonly used pork fat, but with a farce specially prepared to suit the delicate aroma of the grouse meat.

The guests received excellent wines which were suited to the character of the dishes and most likely came from Spain. The king quenched his thirst with spring water.

Everybody sat down to the table at three in the afternoon, which is a surprising time of day for us, being too late for luncheon (we remember the French culinary preferences of Stanislaus Augustus) and too early for dinner. We can assume that this odd hour was adapted to the numerous activities of the host and guests.

The dinner lasted long, sometimes until six in the evening, especially if the accompanying discussion was interesting. Therefore the menu had to consist of many courses and had to have variety. But it is difficult to reconstruct them today because the participants of the Thursday dinners had more important matters and problems to consider than passing on to posterity the menus of these intellectual repasts.

The ending of the dinner was staged with discretion. Two pages entered the dining-room. One of them gave the king three fresh plums on a porcelain plate, regardless of the time of year, the second one, a sealed envelope on a silver tray with the written words: *Au Roi*. The royal gardener, who administered the famous orangery in which tropical fruits were grown, knew the secret of preserving fresh plums even through the whole winter. And as for the envelope, the king never opened it, as it contained a blank piece of paper.

Since there were different guests each time, Stanislaus Augustus was always very well informed about what was happening in artists' studios and scientists' laboratories, as well as about the capital's latest news, gossip and moods.

We know the names of some of the guests who frequented these dinners. One of those who was very warmly welcomed was the outstanding poet Ignacy Krasicki, Bishop of Warmia, who was distinguished by his elegant manners and his wit. The poet-freethinker, titular chamberlain and royal secretary Stanisław Trembecki was also a frequent guest. He was especially favoured by the king, who often saved him from a tight spot by paying off his carelessly acquired debts.

Among the guests of the Thursday dinners the following were held in high esteem by the host: the eminent historian Adam Naruszewicz; the progressive political writer, reformer of education and founder of the Collegium Nobilium*, Stanisław Konarski; the writer of comedies and co-editor of the first Polish newspaper, *Monitor*, Franciszek Bohomolec; the secretary of the National

---

* Collegium Nobilium: a boarding-school for young noblemen founded in 1740, which marked the beginning of the reform of the Polish educational system.

Education Commission and member of the Society for Elementary Books, Grzegorz Piramowicz; the king's former teacher of rhetoric, Antonio Portalupi; the astronomer Stefan Łuskina; the historian, numismatist and archivist Jan Albertrandi; the eminent geographer whose work *The Geography of Present ˙ Times* was withdrawn from public sale on the order of the Russian ambassador in Warsaw Repnin, Karol Wyrwicz; and many others — in other words the intellectual élite of Warsaw and Poland.

The splendid as well as simple food, the guests who represented not a hereditary but an intellectual aristocracy — all of this evoked comments in Warsaw and outside the capital and especially negative comments on the part of the magnates.

However, there were quite a lot of imitators, since the model to follow was not only a good one, but came from above. This was just as the king had wished. No doubt snobbery played a certain role here with Stanislaus Augustus as well as his followers.

The Thursday dinners had much to do with the fact that the cultural and social life of Warsaw was refreshed by the Enlightenment, which penetrated beyond the capital as well.

The king, wanting to raise the general culture of Poland from its Saxon decline, began a war against the widely spread drinking habits. And it can be said that this was one of the few campaigns which he did not lose. The chronicler Łukasz Gołębiowski (1773—1849) who was a direct witness of these efforts, noted with approval:

"During the sober days of Stanislaus Augustus, as a result of better education, nobler examples and sentiments, drinking has ceased."

The humorous curse thrown at the king-abstainer by one of the heroes of *Monachomachia* is very significant. It was expressed by the monk-drunkard Eliseus, into whose mouth Ignacy Krasicki put these words:

O you, who sit on the Polish throne,

You have scorned mead and dislike wine!
You don't mind if drinking dies out
You prefer books, and leave cellars in ruins,
You have plundered the nation of goblets, glasses and
barrels,
May you never become drunk in your life.

The outstanding historian and patriot Joachim Lelewel (1786—1861) looked back on the achievements of Stanislaus Augustus in the field of Polish culture from a certain distance:

"With a great effort he assembled a library, gathered antiques, prints, surrounded himself with scholars, gave out medals to those who brought credit to science and rewards whenever he could. At the open table kept each Thursday he gathered scholars for unceremonious meetings..."

At these "open tables" the king's favourite, lamb, was very often served in the exquisite "interpretations" of master Paweł Tremo. And so we supplement our tale about the Thursday dinners with a few recipes for the mutton dishes adapted by the Polish cuisine.

Saddle of Mutton in Cream

This is a very elegant way of serving mutton, which has a taste similar to venison. The fine saddle must be thoroughly cleaned of fat and the edges should be trimmed a little. Place the saddle in a dish and cover with a boiling marinade made from one cup of light ale, one cup of vinegar and one cup of water and a large sliced onion, 10 grains of pepper, 10 grains of pimento (allspice), 1 bay leaf and 20 dried juniper berries. Marinate the saddle in a cool place for 3—4 days.

One hour before roasting remove saddle from the marinade, dry with a clean cloth, rub with salt and dust sparingly with coarsely ground pepper. Place the pan with the saddle in a hot oven, from time to time basting it with melted butter. When nicely browned, remove part of the fat from the pan, dust the meat with flour and cover with 3/4 pint sour cream. The total roasting time for the saddle is about two hours. Before serving, check if the sauce is salty enough. Arrange the portioned saddle on a platter and pour sauce over it. Besides mashed potatoes or dry-roasted rice, beets may be served, lightly seasoned with garlic but without sour cream, or simmered red cabbage, or lettuce seasoned with oil and lemon juice (but not with sour cream!).

Roast Mutton Stuffed with Ham

This is a very elegant dish and is not more costly than other roasts, at the same time being easy to prepare.

Remove the fat from a large slice of mutton (from the shoulder or leg), weighing about 2 lbs. Pound into a thin slice, taking care not to pierce the meat. Dust the meat with salt and pepper and rub with 2 garlic cloves finely minced to a pulp. When pounding the meat, try to form it into the shape of a square.

Cover the meat evenly with farce, folding up the edges, then roll it tightly and tie it liberally with a cotton thread (previously scalded in boiling water!).

Brown the roll on all sides in hot butter (4 oz.) Next, cover the pan and roast in a hot oven, from time to time basting it with a tablespoon of cream (using 1/2 cup of slightly soured fresh and not yet completely thickened cream).

Farce: Grind in a meat grinder 6 oz. ham (cooked), 2 oz. dried bread that has been soaked in milk and then well squeezed out and 2 oz. raw beef-bone marrow. The marrow may be substituted with butter (2 oz.), which is added to the ground ham and bread.

Separately, fry 1 finely chopped onion in 1 tablespoon butter, not allowing it to brown. By hand knead the mixture of ground ham with bread and marrow, fried onion along with the fat in which it was fried, a large teaspoon of finely minced parsley and a large raw egg, into a farce of even consistency. The farce may be varied by adding to it 4 oz. finely chopped champignons that have been fried with an onion.

Roast Mutton Wild Game Style No. 1

Remove excess suet from 3 lbs. boneless mutton cut from the leg. Place in a stoneware pot or enamelled dish and cover with cooled marinade, prepared in the following way: in a small saucepan bring to the boil 1/2 cup dry red wine with the juice of 1 large lemon, along with 10 grains of pepper, 10 grains of pimento (allspice), 3 small bay leaves, 18 dried juniper berries and a pinch of fried rosemary or several fresh rosemary leaves. The meat, covered with the marinade and kept in a cool place, must be turned over twice a day. After three days the meat is ready for roasting.

Lard the meat with pork fat (2 oz.) or, having rubbed it with salt, roll it in thin strips of pork fat and tie with a cotton thread. Dust the larded meat with flour. Heat intensely 4 oz. butter in a cast-iron pan, then place the meat into this and, leaving the pan uncovered, brown evenly on all sides.

Slice thinly or cut into small slivers 1 peeled celeriac, 1 carrot, 1 large onion (if desired, a small garlic clove may be added) and place in pan under the browned meat. After pouring 2—3 tablespoons marinade over the roast, stew it, covered, continually adding a little marinade. If there is not enough marinade and the meat is still not tender, broth or water may be added.

Take out the tender roast and after 5—10 minutes cut it into slices that are not too thin. Put the sauce through a sieve. Place the sliced meat into the pan, heat, arrange on a platter and cover with sauce.

Some like to add a tablespoon of drained capers to the sauce after it has been put through the sieve (a sauce that is too thick may be thinned down with 2—3 tablespoons broth). In this case the sauce must be boiled along with the capers.

Roast Mutton Wild Game Style No. 2

Remove suet thoroughly from 3 lbs. well dried, "matured" mutton from the leg. Over this pour boiling marinade made from 3 tablespoons water, the juice of 1 lemon, 10 lightly ground juniper berries and 10 grains each of pepper and pimento (allspice). Place the meat in a cool place and turn over often, lightly rubbing in the marinade. Next day, drain, rub with a ground garlic clove and salt — and after one hour dust with flour and place in a pan with intensely heated butter. When the meat is nicely browned on all sides, place the pan, uncovered, in a hot oven. While roasting, baste frequently with its own sauce. After 30 minutes, place in pan 2 sliced onions, 2—3 dried mushrooms, 5 grains each of juniper, pepper and pimento and add a wine-glass (1/4 pint) dry red wine. Cover the pan and place in oven again. After 60—80 minutes the roast should be just right. If the sauce evaporates too quickly, a little boiling water may be added from time to time. Pour 1/2 cup sour cream over the tender roast and simmer in covered pan for 5 minutes, not longer.

Cut the roast into slices that are not too thin and arrange on a previously warmed platter and over this pour the concentrated sauce (check if it is not too salty!), which has been put through a sieve and to which the mushrooms cut into thin strips have been added.

Serve with dry-roasted rice, beets and mashed potatoes.

Beets for Roast Mutton and Game

Beets are usually served flavoured with sour cream. However, they are prepared in a slightly different way for roast mutton, without cream.

Grate coarsely 2 lbs. washed, cooked and peeled beets.

Separately, lightly brown 1 oz. flour with 1 finely chopped onion in 2 oz. butter. The onion may also be fried in pork fat and when it becomes glassy, the flour is added. Thin down the mixture with 1/2 cup broth, bring to a boil and add grated beets and one garlic clove minced to a pulp. Simmer this over low heat for a while, then salt to taste and add a pinch of sugar. Before serving, flavour the beets slightly with lemon juice or else with dry red wine, but then they must be simmered once more for 10 minutes before serving. When serving the beets with roasts without a sauce or in their own scant sauce, they may be seasoned with sour cream.

The aromas coming from the royal kitchen spread through all of Warsaw, since every novelty arouses interest and becomes a subject of comments and gossip. The royal cook, Paweł Tremo, was a popular personality in Warsaw. He was much admired and was doubtless influential. But he was not the only one so popular.

The Warsaw of the second half of the 18th century could boast of other master chefs, not only foreigners but Poles as well. The demand for cooks familiar with new culinary trends was considerable, and experienced chefs trained young and able Poles in this noble and difficult art.

Such a training lasted for several years and if the youth showed diligence and talent, the effort was rewarded by the diploma of master chef, called a "patent". The trainee had to begin at the lowest level, and go through the stages of being an attendant, then a cook's boy, a cook of cooked dishes, roasts etc., until finally mastering the secrets of confectionery art.

The pupil had to make notes of everything that he learnt in his everyday activities. These notes, called *seksterna*, were checked by the master chef himself, who corrected or added something if the need arose. Care was taken that the future culinary master learn to appreciate order and cleanliness. Czerniecki in his *Compendium Ferculorum* already makes demands in this matter which do not differ much from the demands of today: "The cook is to be clean, with his crop of hair neatly combed and shaven at the back, his hands washed, his nails cut, a white apron fastened around him, sober, not quarrelsome, humble, nimble, understanding taste well, knowing the needs of the dishes well, and serving everybody well."

Finally, the day arrived when the apprenticeship was over. The candidate had to prepare a feast by himself for his master and for the examination commission. He was allowed to use the aid of only the helpers and cook's boys still in training. Usually he covered the expenses of the feast by himself, but sometimes he had some financial help from the master or the person who had paid for his training.

The master, along with the commission, checked the order and quality of the courses, sometimes suggesting that a seasoning be added or with discretion recommending the removal of an unsuccessful dish. The commission also looked over the *seksterna* of the candidate and determined whether they were complete. Thus, the master chef's "dissertation" consisted of a written and "oral" examination.

If everything went well, the candidate was called in towards the end of the feast and the commission at the table drank the health of the new associate, presenting him with the master's "patent" on a silver tray. If the new chef had his education financed by a wealthy nobleman, he went on a short training journey abroad, usually to France, at his patron's expense.

One of the diplomas, bestowed in Warsaw in 1783, was signed among others by maître d'hôtel Paweł Tremo, Jacek Tremo, Jean T. Duchesnoy and Franciszek Bielecki.

The young master chef who had a "patent" found work at once. It was usually well paid, not only in private houses, but also in the quickly multiplying restaurants in Warsaw.

The most fashionable and of course the most expensive was the White Eagle Hotel, famous for its excellent food. Only the rich, wealthy noblemen, foreign merchants and diplomats passing through Warsaw stayed here.

In the Old Town there were numerous eating-places known as *traktiernie* (trattoria). In 1754 there were five. Prices there were moderate and the food was good and varied. They were visited by the gentry that came to the city and by the burghers. But the truly democratic places were the numerous and very prosperous *garkuchnie* (cook-shops). One could have an inexpensive and tasty meal there, the menu consisting mostly of traditional Polish dishes that were substantial and well prepared. Some of these *garkuchnie* began specializing in the preparation of only specific dishes, e.g. tripe, bigos or pork roast. These *garkuchnie*, which were not shunned by the poorer folk either, were the eating-places not only for the lesser gentry, but for the artisans and craftsmen as well.

The well-supplied buffet at the theatre was very popular, being elegant, but also expensive. However, the costliest buffets were at masked balls, where the prices and quality were higher than those of the White Eagle Hotel.

Bottled beer, cakes, candy and fruit were served even in the Seym during its sessions.

Thus Warsaw eating-places were developing very successfully in the days of King Stanislaus.

However, we know less about the Warsaw coffee-houses of those times. In the beginning, during the Saxon years, there were few of them. But as early as 1822 there were more than 90 (!). Some of them were especially popular, e.g. in 1790 Okuniowa's coffee-house, which was soon outshone by Neybertowa's "Village Coffee". This was a suburban café then, in which aside from exquisite coffee, other delicacies were served. It consisted of seven rooms, which barely had enough space for its numerous guests. A lasting trace has been left by this café in the name of Wiejska (Village) street, situated near today's Seym.

The atmosphere of the city was particularly favourable to the setting up of these coffee-houses, for it was here that the latest political news at home and abroad was passed on, that discussions were held and appointments made for more confidential conversation. It was here that the top publicists of the Polish Enlightenment met, forming a "group of pens", significantly called Kołłątaj's Forge (Kuźnica Kołłątajowska) by political opponents. Thus some of the Warsaw cafés had their steady customers for whom usually a separate, secluded room was reserved, which enabled them to have discussions without any witnesses. The popularity of coffee in Poland during the Enlightenment can be seen in the fact that the importation of coffee, generally through Gdańsk, amounted to 2,130,000 lbs. towards the end of the 18th century!

Coffee altogether changed the traditional Polish breakfast, which until then had as its base the hot and substantial beer soup. According to the testimony of Father Jędrzej Kitowicz:

"When coffee had become a custom, an artisan bought coffee that was already ground and roasted in a shop with spices for six *groszy*, some rock sugar for another six *groszy*, half a gallon of milk for a third six *groszy*; in this milk he heated the coffee, gave everyone a piece of the rock sugar, which was put in the mouth and the coffee drunk through it, each sip being followed by thin slices of bread with butter. And in this way he had his own breakfast as well as that of his wife, children, servants, up to a few persons, for a sum which before had been sufficient for one or two at the most."

The coffee was thin, of course, often adulterated with roasted acorns and chicory. In cafés and more affluent private homes the coffee was excellent, aromatic and strong. The rock sugar was also considerably cheaper than the imported, snow-white cane sugar sold in loaves. The latter was still an elegant condiment, since in 1784 the Jewish *Kahal* presented King Stanislaus Augustus, who was passing through Kobryń, with... a sugarloaf. There is even an old Polish proverb: "The king is a great lord, but even he does not eat sugar by the spoonfuls."

During the reign of Stanislaus Augustus, just as today, Warsaw was extremely fond of sweets, especially when the old desserts were enriched with oriental, Turkish novelties.

The visit of the Turkish envoy Nauman Bey, from August 1777 to March 1778, became a real festival of refined Turkish confectionery art. This was the last Turkish mission before the partitions of Poland. The envoy, who was magnificently received and lavishly presented with gifts by the king and magnates, reciprocated this not only by presenting costly gifts, but also by inviting his hosts to his Warsaw residence for "Turkish receptions", during which ice-cream, lemonades, sherbets, preserves, various sweets and cakes, coffee Turkish style and pipes were served. The political result of this mission was minimal, but it left a permanent sweet trace in Polish cooking.

During King Stanislaus' period we can speak of the development of the burgher cuisine. In essence it remained faithful to the Old Polish traditions and did not differ much from the cuisine of the middle gentry, which used mainly home-bred and home-made products. And these were plentiful in the villages and, thanks to the resourceful merchants and good salesmen, at the market place and in stalls throughout the city.

Everyday dinners were also bountiful and tasty. They opened with a favourite Polish soup, such as borsch, broth, *krupnik* (barley soup), *kapuśniak* (cabbage soup) or *grochówka* (pea soup). The poorer folk did not eat meat every day, but the wealthier burghers treated themselves to a meat dish after the soup: boiled beef, *zrazy*, variously prepared *kiełbasa* (Polish sausage), tripe and *kishkas* (blood sausages). Kasha was an addition to meat dishes, although potatoes also had their advocates. Cooked cabbage or sauerkraut was also served, generously flavoured with butter or lard. Other vegetables were beets, the universally popular dried peas with cabbage, a favourite dish of the burghers, gentry and the common people, especially when fat smoked bacon was added liberally. Carrots, beans and turnips were also eaten. On Lent days there was fish and salt herring on the less wealthy tables.

The suppers were plentiful as well, though more modest than the dinners. Kashas were eaten, as well as various noodles and dumplings, vegetables liberally flavoured with butter or lard, cold meats, less frequently meat. For supper beer was served, which was valued for its ability to bring sleep after a hard day's work.

Roasts, chicken, duck, goose and desserts were mostly Sunday or holiday dishes.

This is more or less how the burghers and artisans of Warsaw ate. On occasions such as important holidays and family celebrations the meals were more sumptuous.

The tables of wealthy patricians, merchants and bankers, when the occasion demanded, were not worse supplied than those of the magnates. On such occasions there were salads, peas, mushrooms, asparagus, very costly truffles brought over from France, and such exquisite fruit as apricots, peaches and even oranges. Many fine fruits were grown in the royal orangery, and in the hothouses of the magnates there were even pineapples, figs and oranges. Thanks to the contacts kept up, these rare and costly fruits doubtless found their way to the tables of the patricians, especially the bankers, since money drew together people of different backgrounds.

Warsaw's artisans were deservedly popular in Poland and often people came from far away to do their shopping in the capital. Some artisans made modest fortunes, usually employing several helpers in their workshops and living quite well. There were even times when they presented gifts to King Stanislaus Augustus on certain occasions. For example the well-known baker of Warsaw, Szyler, presented a gigantic strudel to the king on the first anniversary of his accession to the throne. "It was 7 ells long, as the king had been elected on 7 September, the flour was taken from 17 mills, because the king was born on 17 January, there were 32 various seasonings, in accordance with the king's age, the enormous strudel was carried by the 9 children of Szyler, since September, in which the election had taken place, was the ninth month of the year." The king rewarded the baker and his children generously and presented the strudel to the Bernardine monastery. Szyler must have been a master of high class, because what baker of today would dare to bake such a giant when cakes of much smaller size are sometimes unsuccessful.

Foreigners who visited the capital praised the Warsaw —
and in general the Polish — cuisine of the end of the
18th century.

J.E. Biester, in his *Letters on Poland* (1791) did not omit
culinary matters when writing the following:

"Maybe too much attention is paid to food here, although
in this case Poles show common sense and good taste. All
travellers admit that there are three excellent important
products in Poland: bread, wine and coffee... Good,
strong coffee is called Polish coffee here as well as in
neighbouring countries, and bad coffee is called German.
Similarly, old, strong Hungarian wine is called Polish wine,
and heavy sweet wine, German."

Biester came in touch mainly with the burgher cuisine
and ate in Warsaw's *traktiernias*, and perhaps even in the
somewhat snobbish White Eagle. The food must have been
good if a foreigner considered it to be very good.

Old Polish unlimited appetites were curbed and slowly
transformed into more moderate gourmet appetites. The
borderline between the cuisine of the gentry and the
burghers began to fade in those days. Here and there one
could still find some extravagance of the magnates, but
they aroused criticism rather than admiration.

But neither rationalism nor even the most progressive or
radical social and political opinions need exclude the joys
that good cooking gives. The burghers and artisans of King
Stanislaus' days gave an example of this. They attained
some more rights and privileges for themselves (unfortunately not for long) that were enough to show that if the
state wanted to exist and develop, it had to provide
protection for them and not weigh them down with
ruinous burdens. This was expressed in the pamphlet by
Franciszek Salezy Jezierski (1740—91), *A Voice in Haste
to the Burgher Estate* written with an excellent journalistic
flair.

In 1786 the cookbook entitled *The Perfect Cook* was
published in Warsaw, then reprinted and emended several

times. It was not an original work, but translated from the French. Subsequent editions, with Polish recipes added, are more interesting for the student of Old Polish cuisine than the original edition, in which there are mostly French recipes that were costly and probably not too often tried out by housewives.

In the year 1812, when the famous "last Old Polish feast" took place, created in the 12th chapter of *Pan Tadeusz* by the brilliant pen of Adam Mickiewicz, the anonymous author of *The Perfect Cook with Exquisite Taste*, following the revolutionary trends coming from France, designed his work for "the convenience of Citizens and Citizen-Housewives", in other words for Polish "citoyens" and not for the gentry-magnate élite.

In the chapter dealing with beef we read the quite significant words:

"In the houses of burghers, that is of people who like to eat well, one takes..." (here follows a list of the best parts of a beef carcass). The author calls other parts of beef, not mentioned in the list, "base meat which is used by the common people. It is seasoned with salt, pepper, vinegar, garlic and shallots in order to give it a better flavour". The "common people" were the townsfolk, who liked to eat well, as is seen from the list of seasonings above.

The book described above was prepared, according to the author, is a manner "suitable for frugality". For us, who read this book, it is an example of astonishing extravagance, but it is a known fact that frugality was understood differently in various periods.

Some recipes are called: "city style", "peasant style" and suggest the flavour of home-cooking. But most dishes, of typically foreign origin, are presented by the author in the following versions: French style, German style, English style, Spanish style, Italian style, Genoese, Sultan style, Turkish style, Lyonnaise, à la St. Ménéhoult, à la Robert, etc. In some recipes there are truffles, Swiss cheese, Parmesan, in many wine, in one recipe turtles.

One may doubt whether the burghers of Warsaw or other Polish towns ate so richly, but it is certain that they did eat well. Unfortunately, such items as *Compendium Ferculorum*, or the successfully preserved manuscript of the maître d'hôtel Paweł Tremo, have not been reprinted yet, even in bibliophile editions. Therefore, we shall reconstruct the picture of an Old Polish table by basing ourselves mainly on literary sources, memoirs, chronicles, epigrams and on a very valuable source — the opinions of foreigners who visited Poland. It is they who, by comparing the Polish way of cooking with that of other nations, underlined its distinct character, originality and variety as well as its high quality and even its superiority.

Even though the king showed a great fondness for anything French not only in the intellectual sphere, but in culinary matters as well, the journal *Monitor*, of excellent editorship and published at Stanislaus Augustus' initiative, warned against the excessive imitation of foreign models and the omission of national dishes.

"A cook who is unacquainted with French concoctions and scorns borsch, broth and bigos, is made to fry supposedly foreign delicacies..."

A particularly painful and irretrievable loss for the student and admirer of Old Polish cooking are the countless, almost totally lost, little books written by hand by housewives and containing specialities of the house. Preserved with care and supplemented throughout the years, they too fell prey to the last wars. Perhaps some of these "culinary jewels" have survived and are now lying disregarded in attics among useless junk destined for destruction. If only a small portion of them could be saved!

Biester rightly noted that during King Stanislaus' days much attention was given to food in Poland. Even too much attention was given if one compares Polish culinary customs with the thrifty German way of cooking, as Biester admits himself. The preoccupation with good food was connected, as it still is, with the innate hospitality of Poland where guests have always been welcomed with joy, and treated with the best from pantry and cellar.

Let us listen to Łukasz Gołębiowski for a while. He lived at the turn of the 18th and 19th centuries and knew Polish hospitality not from books, but from personal experience:

"The main principle of the Polish way of life is hospitality; a Pole does not like eating alone, be it an everyday meal, or something better; hence his joy at seeing a guest; when there is no family he must have a house-guest, a resident, he will call for the parish-priest, for it is more pleasant to eat and enjoy conversation in company.

"Among the lower estates too, when someone slaughters a pig, catches some game or fish, has some fresh early vegetables, he soon invites company or sends out the news and his hospitality is reciprocated with equal politeness. And it is not to make an impression only, nor for any prospects that our compatriot acts thus: he has, so to say, imbibed hospitality at the breast, from the earliest years in the house of his parents and has seen its examples everywhere. Can it therefore ever be abandoned?"

As for the Old Polish cuisine, which was still simply Polish cuisine for him, he writes:

"And so although we have gladly assimilated the dishes of almost every country — borrowing from the Russians, Turks, Swedes, Germans, French, English, Italians and Spaniards — we have preserved our national traditions giving preference to our national dishes; we miss them when abroad and at the most elaborate tables our compatriot yearns for them and would happily return to borsch, *kapuśniak* and *bigos*."

Thus when many Poles had to look for shelter abroad, especially in France, after the defeat of Napoleon's Moscow campaign and after the repression of the 1830 and 1863 insurrections:

"The more wealthy in Paris have Polish cooks; the military officers in Chantilly, Spain and Italy trained their countrymen to cook their favourite delicacies for them."

Everything that Gołębiowski says is moving and very true. Even though over one hundred years have passed since these words were written, they are still basically topical:

"A Pole is always polite, open, sincere, a friend to anyone whom he calls to the table...; without the fair sex and politeness towards it, there is no feast for a Pole.

"He will not treat you only when he needs your vote. Who is a stranger or family to our compatriot? of kin or not? a friend or a foe? an acquaintance or an unknown person? superior or inferior? Which of these did not find an open table or hand, a sincere reception, forgetfulness of all grievances? How many times has he not treated those who would never return his favours, whom he would never see again?"

And, ending this praise of Polish hospitality. he adds: "We can recognize this with pride and pass on to our children this precious heritage, this beautiful custom."

One could easily compile a thick volume on the praises of Polish hospitality, written by foreigners visiting Poland for various reasons in the past ages. It has not been done thus far, since even today hospitality seems to be something so natural to Poles that it almost does not deserve mention.

Therefore, in a way, a Pole might be called stingy: he would stint himself in order to share with another.

Just as the Polish cuisine preserved its national character in spite of culinary fashions that did not affect its roots, the way in which a table was set, while assimilating the widespread new fashions, also preserved its Polish character — not only on the surface.

Instead of splendid and massive silverware, which was gold-plated and sometimes even of real gold, faience appeared on the Polish tables, to be followed by porcelain. This change did not come about suddenly, during the reign of Stanislaus Augustus. Already during the days of John III Sobieski, Chinese and even Japanese porcelain was collected and very high prices were paid for it. But it served only as decoration, being placed on console tables or in glass cases, where it was protected against breakage.

During the times of the Saxon kings faience and porcelain decidedly appeared on Polish tables. At the beginning, faience was expensive, elaborately painted, usually imported from from Faenza in Italy. The new article was costly and servants as well as participants of the repast had to accustom themselves to handling these fragile, easily breakable dishes, platters and plates with extra care.

Porcelain was somewhat more resistant and at the same time more elegant. Saxon porcelain made in Meissen quickly gained great popularity among the wealthy. Complete sets of tableware in a uniform style could be imported from Meissen for any number of persons. These included soup tureens, salad bowls, sauceboats, saltcellars and beautiful candle holders. A table laid with the porcelain looked beautiful, especially as silver dishes were also placed on it. These were light and of a fashionable shape, often repeating the shape of the porcelain dishes. However, porcelain was predominant. The older, more massive silverware, which the magnates still possessed in great amounts, decorated the sideboard for many years, giving testimony of the wealth of the house.

The silver "services" described earlier, which decorated the centre of the nobleman's table, did not fall into disuse too quickly, since *The Perfect Cook* (1812 edition), when giving the dinner menu for 15—20 persons, clearly recommends: "1 silver or other service in the centre, which is to remain through all the courses".

While silver tableware became outdated, silver cutlery was retained on the wealthier tables, although the handles were also of porcelain.

Poland had considerable silver deposits of its own worked in the famous mines near Olkusz till the end of the 18th century. There were also excellent goldsmiths, the best ones coming from Lvov and Cracow. Their work was highly valued outside of Poland. It should be added that Polish goldsmith traditions go back to the 17th—18th centuries, and that during the times of King Stanislaus Polish silverware was known for its high artistic level and the great care taken in the finishing touches.

During the Saxon period there were cups and goblets made of glass on Polish tables. These were only partly a novelty since Polish glass has traditions that go back to the early Middle Ages. The oldest Polish glazier's workshop, found in Kruszwica, is believed to date back to the 12th—13th centuries. In the 16th century there were 30 glass factories. But during the Saxon days glassware was usually imported, mainly from Bohemia.

During the reign of Stanislaus Augustus the first workshops that produced faience and table glass came into being. Their life span was generally very short, even though they hold a distinguished place in the history of the Polish ceramic industry. The political situation in Poland was not favourable to the durability of the king's praiseworthy initiatives even in this field. And yet the Polish faience, porcelain and glass of King Stanislaus' era managed to attain amazingly quickly a level so high, that they could well compete with imported products.

The Warsaw workshop at the Belvedere palace set up by the king (open 1768—83) at first manufactured porcelain, but soon as a result of a lack of the appropriate raw material, turned to faience. And even though the Belvedere faience goods were true works of art, the royal *farfurnia* lost money. The king had to subsidize each item by as much as its sale price. The few Belvedere pieces which have been preserved arouse admiration for their fine workmanship and especially for the exquisite painting that decorates them. The workshop produced two sets famous among connoisseurs: the Sultan's set, consisting of 160 pieces, and the royal set, made to order for Stanislaus Augustus' own use. The first was offered by the king to Sultan Abdul-Hamid I. Less than twenty pieces have survived from both sets.

The wares manufactured in Korzec in the years 1784—1832 are also very rare and sought after by collectors today. As opposed to the Belvedere ware, faience and porcelain from Korzec found numerous buyers. In the years of its greatest development 20,000 pieces of porcelain and faience left the factory each year, decorating even the modest tables of the gentry and burghers. The wares from Korzec were also exported abroad with great success. They had their own Polish decorative style (for example, Volhynian landscape, wild flowers etc. were painted on the dishes). There were other Polish workshops and factories, some of them working well into the 19th century, that produced beautiful faience and porcelain.

The factory of faience and porcelain in Ćmielów, established in 1809 and converted into a porcelain factory in 1842, is working to this day and manufactures porcelain sought after throughout the world. The products of the faience factory in Włocławek also go back to the beautiful traditions of Polish faience.

18th century Polish glass must also be mentioned here. Thanks to glasses and goblets, the wine hitherto drunk from silver cups revealed one of its great attractions: its colour.

The most famous glass came from Urzecz from the middle of the 18th till the middle of the 19th century. The glass factory there manufactured not only a large selection of elegantly shaped and artistically engraved glasses and goblets, but also unusually decorative candle holders and mirrors of such fine lustre and elegant frames, that they bore comparison with Venetian mirrors. There was also beautiful Polish crystal, manufactured in the crystal factory established in Huciska in 1717.

The Polish table of the second half of the 18th century, with its display of porcelain, glass, crystal and candle holders, must have been a true feast to the eye.

Although this is a picture of a rich lord's table, the lesser gentry and burghers were not prepared either to sit down to a carelessly laid table. They had a clean linen tablecloth, beautifully painted faience and later porcelain plates (since Polish porcelain was much cheaper and just as attractive as imported porcelain) and serving platters for their favourite dishes — all of which made up a picture pleasing to the eye on ordinary days, not to mention times when the table was set for a holiday or for guests. These were occasions for more pompous displays, but Poles did this *con amore*, adhering to the principle that "a thaler's worth of damage is better than half a *groszy* of disgrace".

We have already described the "Polish feast" made up of Polish products solely, given by chancellor Ossoliński. During the days of Stanislaus Augustus Polish dishes and drinks could be served on Polish porcelain and in Polish glass, on a beautiful Polish tablecloth, using silverware made of Polish silver.

The days of King Stanislaus thus had their glories, aside from the menacing shadows drawing in.

In our tale some mention should also be made of music, since it accompanied many a repast from primaeval times on and embellished social life.

The Polish peasantry are exceptionally musical. They have created thousands of songs that accompany rites, family celebrations and everyday work. Songs were one of the most important elements of the colourful village weddings. A testimony to the wealth of Polish folk songs and dances are the more than 60 volumes collected by Oskar Kolberg (1814—90) entitled *The Village Folk. Its Customs, Way of Life, Speech, Legends, Sayings, Rites, Witchcraft, Games, Songs, Music and Dances*, containing over ten thousand melodies.

Gallus Anonymous writes that music resounded in the homes of the wealthy as early as the dawn of the Piast era. We know that in later ages numerous and often excellent bands of musicians played before the king, in the homes of magnates and noblemen and even in towns. Bands of musicians were also to be found in churches and monasteries. They served as entertainment, accompanied repasts and dances. Those who could not afford their own musicians, brought over musicians from the city in order to add glamour to a wedding or any other festivity. In the memoirs of the nobleman Zawisza, dated 1710, we read: "...I had fine music from Minsk, with a dulcimer, they played old-fashioned dances well."

The gentry took up music less frequently, as the "craft" of a musician just like other crafts was considered not worthy of those highly-born. But though Łukasz Górnicki (1527—1603) writes in *The Polish Courtier* that "our gentry rarely play the violin or the fife", social life could not do without music. On the other hand, the gentry, particularly young girls, enjoyed playing the lute, whether for the mood or as an accompaniment to songs or dances. Numerous lutanists, theorbists and later Cossack bandore players became famous in noblemen's manor-houses. The nobleman himself liked to reach for the theorbo in order to play in a closed family circle or among friends.

During repasts at the table, the musicians were seated on a special gallery above the dining-room. They were not always of a high standard. In modest village manors situated far away from the bigger towns, peasant musicians who also played in the numerous public houses were often engaged. Jewish musicians, who mostly played the dulcimer and violin, were much liked. Jews in fact were valued musicians and were among the court musicians of King Ladislaus Jagiello.

The music that accompanied repasts was rather discreet, not disturbing the conversation. This quiet, pleasant music was called *gędźba* or *gędzenie*. Only the toasts. were accompanied by a noisy *tutti* of the whole band.

"The horn screamed behind your ear, the drums were pounded upon like a box, until your head split," complained Mikołaj Rej, which we, people living in the pop song era, harassed by city bustle, the noise of cars and roar of jet planes, understand only too well.

Music was also practised in monasteries, which kept their own musicians who played not only during religious rites, but also in refectories to make festive meals more pleasant, for example on the holiday of the patron saint. The famous book of organ music of Jan of Lublin, a monk and organist in a monastery in Kraśnik near Lublin, which was written in the first half of the 16th century, aside from church music contains also a rich collection of Polish dances popular in those days.

The burghers were very fond of music as well and they usually showed better taste and musical cultivation than the gentry. City musicians, who played *ex arte*, that is from notes, formed the oldest guild in Poland during the reign of Casimir the Great. In time each greater town had its own guild of musicians and a group that played on town festivities and in burgher houses. The royal chapel was particularly privileged, which is seen in the fact that in 1440 its members did not come under the jurisdiction of the town court of justice, but under the starost's court. Musicians belonging to guilds did not favour the activities of minstrels, who were wandering students *(clerici vagabundi)* and very popular among the lower ranks.

In the inventories of wealthy burgher families we meet numerous musical instruments, which shows that music was enjoyed in the home. The ability to play the currently most popular "salon" instrument was part of the good upbringing required of the daughters of noblemen and burghers.

This was Old Polish entertainment music, of which more descriptions than scores have survived.

With time, some folk dances acquired the high status of national dances. These were the polonaise, mazurka, cracovienne, *oberek* and *kujawiak*. The polonaise conquered Europe in the 18th century, and became really popular, particularly in Germany. Johann Philipp Kirnberger (1721—83), a pupil of the great Johann Sebastian Bach, who became acquainted with Polish polonaises and mazurkas during his long stay in Poland, wrote that Polish polonaises differed as much from the polonaises composed in great quantities in Germany then, as "a priest from a grave-digger, even though both are dressed in black". The excellent German composer Georg Philipp Telemann (1681—1767) was a great enthusiast of Polish folk music. He admitted openly that it was a boundless source of inspiration for him.

And so, when we speak of Old Polish hospitality, customs, cuisine and repasts, we cannot omit the music that we call entertainment music today. It flourished in the royal chambers as well as in village manors, residences of the magnates and peasant cottages, in the homes of the burghers as well as in public houses. Poles were very fond of it and it added an irreplaceable flavour to a pleasant life without aspiring to the ranks of great art. It was a comfort in times of troubles of the heart and a faithful companion to happier days.

Christmas

Christmas is the most festive

holiday in Poland next to Easter. This holiday is for the
family and is usually celebrated in the company of those
dearest to us. Its traditions go back to the pagan Slavic
days. This can be said especially of the Christmas Eve
supper, probably the only Polish festive meal in which the
rites of times earlier than Christianity have been preserved.
In the Polish Christmas both of these threads — the pagan
and the Christian — are interwoven into a colourful,
poetic whole.

People sat down to their Christmas Eve supper at dusk,
at the moment the evening star appeared, which was eagerly
awaited by the children. First, a consecrated wafer was
divided among everybody and greetings were exchanged.
This is a moment more moving than any other in the
year, awakening many childhood recollections. It is
a moment of grief for those who are gone forever and at
the same time a moment of hope for happiness, eternally
burning in human hearts.

For children it is probably the most beautiful evening
in the year, in which the mood of a fairy tale becomes real
for a few hours in the brightness of the lights on the
Christmas tree under which loving hands have placed such
gifts as they could for everyone present. But even the most
modest gift has a special value that evening and becomes
a symbol of the love and friendship that unites people.

Christmas as well as Easter are the culminating points
of the Polish culinary year. But before we look into the
culinary framework of holidays, let us recall some customs
connected with the Polish Christmas.

Many of them are derived from Slavic rites; they have
survived until today, showing how deeply they were rooted
in the hearts of our ancestors.

The 20th century, an age of revolutionary social changes
and technical discoveries, values and respects these echoes
of times long gone by, which are naïve perhaps, but full

of unrepeatable poetry, since there is a spark of yearning for happiness and peace in them.

Today, the largest number of these old customs connected with Christmas have survived in the countryside, although the city has also retained many of them.

In villages there is a custom that unthreshed sheaves of wheat are placed in the room in which the Christmas Eve supper is to take place. They are placed in the four corners, or in the corner to the east. There is an old custom, preserved in some regions, that after Christmas Eve the domestic animals are given a piece of the wafer to ensure them health and fine offspring. It was believed that at midnight animals spoke with a human voice, but overhearing this brought bad luck. In regions especially threatened by wolves, leftovers from the Christmas Eve supper were placed outside the gate to invite the wolves which, when treated so well, would not do the host any harm. Another widespread custom, found in cities as well, is to place hay under the tablecloth that covers the supper table. During supper the young people told their fortunes from the hay. If a green blade of grass was pulled out from under the tablecloth, it meant success in love and a wedding. A blackened blade meant bad luck, unfulfilled marital plans and even spinsterhood. This fortune-telling was not taken too seriously but everyone enjoyed himself very much.

Dividing the wafer, however, has always been a particularly solemn moment. On this festive occasion all wrongs are forgiven and reconciliation is sealed by a kiss.

The dead were also remembered. For "the absent" a separate place was set at the table, at which a little food from every course and a piece of the wafer were placed. Old Polish wafers were multi-coloured and very decorative. Today white wafers are baked, also decorated with an embossed pattern.

Probably the finest Old Polish Christmas custom was to invite the lonely for Christmas Eve supper, because on that particular evening no one should be left alone.

One could carry on and on about Polish Christmas Eve customs, but we have selected only some of them.

Polish Christmas carols, often very old, are real jewels of Polish folk and religious music. There are dance melodies among them, to the rhythm of the mazurka, *oberek,* cracovienne and polonaise. In the lyrics there are humorous, satirical and even social accents. For many Poles living away from their country Christmas carols have been a moving symbol of their Polish identity. Frédéric Chopin expressed his great yearning for Poland by entwining into his *Scherzo in G-flat minor* the sweet lullaby melody of the Polish Christmas carol *Sleep, Jesus, Sleep.*

In Cracow every year a competition is held for the most beautiful Christmas crèche. The hand-made little scenes of the Christ child in the manger with attending figures are displayed before Christmas at the Cracow market square and the exhibits later enrich private and state collections of folk art. Nativity scenes arranged in churches also have long-standing traditions. A display that deserves particular mention is the mechanical crèche in the Capuchin church in Warsaw to which new details are constantly added. Next to the donkey, ox and camels on which the Magi have come, we can also see a tramcar, a train, a bus and even an airplane!

Unfortunately, carollers dressed in various disguises (like the English mummers) and carrying a large colourful star on a stick lighted from inside visit Polish homes less and less often. This is an old custom, well known es early as the 17th century. At that time Cracow students became famous as the best carollers, and they interspersed their singing with witty orations.

And now let us look into an Old Polish kitchen during the time before Christmas.

It is full of bustle. Smells and aromas blend together, creating a strange symphony made up of many flavours that excite the appetite and imagination. Even today, in the small modern kitchens, when the lady of the house has only the often doubtful help from her husband and children, it is a time of unusually intensive culinary creativity. It is true that some traditional Christmas delicacies can be bought ready-made, but they cannot compare to the dishes that are prepared according to recipes passed on from generation to generation.

The main culinary accent of the Polish Christmas has always been Christmas Eve supper. On the days that followed meals were plentiful, but the dishes were not essentially different from the ones served on other holidays or festive occasions.

The cakes baked for Christmas were less varied than Easter cakes. The first place was taken by gingerbread and poppy-seed cakes. There were also plenty of Old Polish *babas* and in addition various cookies, usually spiced.

Christmas Eve supper was a meatless meal. All dishes were prepared with oil or sometimes with butter. Our very Catholic ancestors, even though they observed the meatless and lardless fast so scrupulously, could produce a real treat for the palate in spite of this restriction. It is not strange, therefore, that such Polish fasts were famous outside the country.

In the homes of the wealthier gentry, the burghers and in the well-off monasteries, the Christmas Eve supper consisted of twelve courses, as many as there were Apostles.

Fish dishes were predominant. These were prepared in the most varied ways. The famous carp (or pike) in grey sauce was a must. Sometimes there were so many fish dishes that the traditional number of twelve courses was insufficient. But there was a way out of this: all fish dishes were considered as one course!

Christmas Eve supper began with one of the traditional soups: red borsch with *uszka* (a kind of ravioli), mushroom soup, or — less frequently — almond soup. Borsch, the classical Old Polish soup, was the most popular.

Aside from fish dishes, there were the well-known Old Polish peas with cabbage, dishes from dried mushrooms, compotes from dried fruit, mainly from prunes, *kutia* (a sweet cereal dish) in the eastern parts of Poland, and various cakes. The fast did not exclude alcoholic beverages, but less was drunk on Christmas Eve than on Easter Sunday.

This is how the Poles of older days observed their fast, setting an example to atheists and heretics. Today such Christmas Eve giants of a supper belong to the irretrievable past. We do not have the appetites of our ancestors, on which huge fortunes were sometimes squandered.

But Christmas Eve suppers are still celebrated, for they possess not only poetic traditions, but the atmosphere of family warmth as well. The flavour and ceremony of traditional Christmas Eve dishes have the ability to evoke these feelings, allowing minds to travel back to the past with its memories and to the future with its hopes and dreams.

We shall add some selected Old Polish recipes of Christmas Eve supper dishes to our tale about Christmas. The individual recipes are for 4—5 persons, with the exception of the cake recipes. We have altered them only slightly — reducing the number of spices too liberally used in Old Polish cooking — but carefully retaining their Polish note.

Christmas Eve Borsch

Red beet borsch is the pride of Old Polish cooking. The oldest recipe surviving comes from the beginning of the 16th century. There are two classical versions of red borsch: borsch for the Christmas Eve fast and for Easter, the latter made with meat stock.

Red borsch is on the menus of the most elegant parties in Poland. Both versions of borsch are made with naturally soured beet juice.

The souring of beets is very simple: Carefully wash the red beets (about 3 lbs), peel and slice thinly. Place them in a glass jar and cover completely with barely lukewarm water. Place a slice of whole-wheat bread on top, which hastens the process. Cover the jar with gauze and place in the warmest place in the kitchen. After four or five days carefully remove the foam from the surface and pour the clear, ruby-red soured juice into clean bottles. In tightly corked bottles that are kept in a cool place they can be stored for several months.

Christmas Eve borsch is prepared with the concentrated stock of the following vegetables: celeriac and parsley root, carrots, leeks and 1 onion. Cook the vegetables along with 4 red beets, peeled and sliced thinly, adding 10 grains of black pepper, 2 grains of pimento (allspice) and a small piece of bay leaf. In a separate pot cook 2—3 oz. dried mushrooms (boletus) in two cups of water. Pour both the vegetable and mushroom stocks through a sieve and mix together. Now add an appropriate amount of soured beet juice (3/4 pint juice for about 2 1/2 pints stock). Heat the borsch until it starts to boil, but not more. If the colour of the borsch is not right, it may be corrected with the juice of a fresh beet, grated to a pulp.

Flavour the borsch very carefully. Its final flavour depends on individual preferences. Apart from salt, the taste may be corrected with a little sugar. The acidity may be enhanced with a wine-glass of dry red wine or lemon juice, but never with vinegar. About 1 5 minutes before serving, add a crushed garlic clove, which gives it an interesting taste and aroma.

Uszka are the traditional addition to Christmas Eve borsch. There should be 6—8 uszka for each person. Place the cooked uszka into a soup-tureen and cover with hot borsch. If the borsch is served in cups, small pierożki (a kind of ravioli) filled with mushroom farce, are served separately.

Uszka for Christmas Eve Borsch

Dough: Knead 6 oz. flour with 1 whole egg and a pinch of salt. The dough should be stiffer than for noodles. If it is too stiff, add a little lukewarm water while kneading. Roll the well kneaded dough out thinly and cut into small squares (measuring 1 1/2 by 1 1/2 inches or slightly smaller). The greater the skill of the cook, the smaller the uszka. Place some farce on each square, fold over diagonally, press firmly together, first around the edge, then the two opposite corners of the triangle. Throw the uszka into salted boiling water. They are ready when they come up to the surface.

Farce: Dice very finely the cooked mushrooms from which the stock has been added to the borsch. Fry in butter with a small, finely chopped onion, then blend thoroughly with 1 tablespoon breadcrumbs and 1 whole raw egg. Add salt and pepper to taste.

Crisp Pieroźki for Borsch

The dough is made from 8 oz. flour, 5 oz. butter, 1 small egg or 2 raw egg yolks, 1 tablespoon sour cream and 1/2 teaspoon salt. Mix these ingredients, cutting them in with a knife. Knead quickly into a dough, which should then "rest" in a cool place for 30 minutes. With a wine-glass cut circles from the thinly rolled out dough. Place some mushroom farce on each circle (the farce is prepared according to the recipe for uszka) and form graceful pieroźki from the circles folded in half, firmly pressing their edges together. Arrange the pieroźki on a metal sheet and bake in a hot oven until golden brown. Serve warm immediately or reheated (in oven).

Christmas Eve Mushroom Soup

The Christmas Eve mushroom soup is made without meat stock, just like the Christmas Eve borsch. It is not meant to fill the stomach, but merely to warm it and arouse the appetite. It is made in the following way: Pour 3 1/2 pints lukewarm water over 2—3 oz. dried boletus mushrooms (which have been briefly washed in cold water) and cook, covered, over low heat. When mushrooms soften, add a fair amount of vegetables (celeriac and parsley root, carrots, leeks, onion) and 10 grains of black pepper. After adding the vegetables, cook 25—30 minutes more.

Strain the soup through a fine sieve, salt to taste and, if desired, add some lemon juice. Add cooked mushroom caps sliced into thin strips and łazanki (a kind of noodle), which have been cooked separately.

Christmas Eve Almond Soup

Today this is the least popular Old Polish Christmas Eve soup, although it does have many ethusiasts among the children.

Pour 2 1/2 pints boiling milk over 6 oz. almonds which have been scalded with boiling water, blanched, thoroughly dried and then ground. Cook over low heat for 15 minutes. Place dry-baked rice (one tablespoon per person) into tureen, and cover with hot almond milk. Just before serving, flavour the soup with a raw egg yolk if desired.

Fried Carp

Cut a cleaned carp into portions, then salt. Let these lie for 30 minutes. Next, dredge each portion with flour, dip in lightly beaten (with a fork) egg and sprinkle with breadcrumbs. Fry over moderate heat, in butter, to a light golden brown colour. The fried portions of carp may be placed in a hot oven for a few minutes (in a covered frying pan) if baking is needed. The butter used for frying should not be skimped on, as the fish will brown too much in a scant amount of fat, losing much of its delicate, refined flavour.

Fried carp is probably the simplest, but very delicious dish for Christmas Eve (not only!), exceptionally popular in Polish cooking.

Horseradish is served with fried carp or cabbage with mushrooms. We strongly recommend this excellent, truly Polish combination.

Let us add that for ages carp has been the

number one fish in Polish cooking. It was bred as early as the 13th century and one of the noblest types of this fish was bred in Poland: the famous royal carp.

Some of the fans of this fish say that a scale of the royal carp (served on Christmas Eve), hidden in a wallet, brings money. Alas, we have tried this out in vain only to discover that it is a superstition.

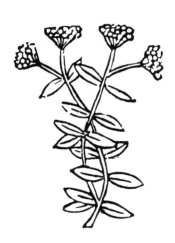

Carp Polish Style in Grey Sauce

This is a famous Old Polish Christmas Eve delicacy. Although it is not so simple, during Christmas we need not always take heed of common sense, which urges us to economize. From the several existing versions of carp in grey sauce we have chosen the one we thought to be most characteristic of Old Polish cooking.

Kill a fine carp of about 2 lbs. and scrupulously collect the blood into a cup which contains the juice of 1/2 lemon.

After cleaning the fish, cut crosswise into portions, salt and leave in a cool place for 20 minutes. Then place the fish in a flat saucepan and cover with the stock (3/4 pint) of 1 medium celeriac root, sliced into strips, a large onion and 1 wine-glass of dry red wine, a piece of thinly peeled lemon rind, several grains of pepper, 1/3 teaspoon ground ginger and the juice of 1/2 lemon. Transfer the cooked fish carefully onto a warm serving-dish and keep warm. Force the stock through a fine metal sieve, add the blood of the carp, a cup of dark beer, 2—3 cubes of sugar, a tablespoon of plum butter, 2 oz. dried and ground gingerbread (baked with honey!), 2 oz. chopped blanched almonds, 2 oz. raisins, and a heaped tablespoon of butter. Simmer this sauce over low heat for 10—15 minutes and when slightly cooler, check the taste (add a little salt if desired). Pour the hot sauce over the fish arranged on the platter.

Pike Jewish Style

This dish, known abroad as pike Polish
style, is a worthy representative of Old
Polish culinary traditions, which made
use of Polish Jewish cooking, known for
its excellent fish dishes.

Clean thoroughly a pike weighing about
2 lbs. Cut crosswise into portions about
1 in. wide. Cut out the meat from each
portion with a sharp knife, taking care not
to pierce the skin. After removing the
bones, chop the pike very finely, adding
10 oz. very finely minced onion, 2 tablespoons breadcrumbs, 1/2 teaspoon sugar,
1 tablespoon grated horseradish and 1 raw
egg white. Mix the above ingredients by
hand into a smooth paste, salt to taste
and arrange tightly on the skin of the
pike, forming the portions into their
original shape. Arrange the filled portions
in a flat saucepan, then cover with the
strained, concentrated stock of cooked
vegetables with 6 grains of black pepper,

5 grains of pimento (allspice) and the remaining parts of the fish (head, bones, tail, fin). Now add to the stock 4 finely sliced large onions, a piece of bay leaf and salt to taste. Cover the pan (not too tightly) and cook the fish over low heat for 1 hour. When the fish is cooked, leave it in the stock until completely cool, then arrange on a platter and cover with the stock with the onion strained through a fine sieve. Leave the platter on the lowest shelf in the refrigerator for a few hours, so that the sauce acquires the consistency of a light jelly.

A glass of Pejsachówka (a kind of plum brandy) goes best with pike Jewish style.

Boiled Pike Perch

Boiled pike perch is a traditional Polish Christmas Eve dish and if two fish dishes are to be served, the first one should be pike perch.

Scale a pike perch (about 2 lbs.), then clean and salt. Prepare a light stock from vegetables (caleriac and parsley root, carrots, leeks), a large onion, a few grains of black pepper and a small piece of bay leaf.

Place the whole fish in a shallow dish for cooking fish and pour the cold stock over so that it covers the fish. Bring to a boil slowly and simmer, covered, over low heat for 15—20 minutes. Leave fish in the stock, not allowing it to cool.

In a saucepan melt 2 oz. butter and when the butter starts to cook, add 3 finely chopped hard-boiled eggs and a tablespoon of minced green parsley. Do not fry, just heat well! Carefully place the hot fish on a warmed up platter, sprinkle evenly with the juice of 1/2 lemon and with the hot mixture of butter, eggs and parsley.

According to connoisseurs, this is the simplest way of serving pike perch. It accentuates the refined flavour and aroma of this noble fish.

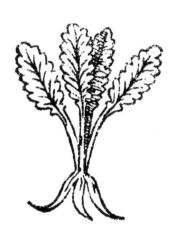

Cabbage with Mushrooms and Nut Croquettes

This dish is an example of good traditional Polish cooking. It seems very plain at first glance, but thanks to the croquettes it becomes original and attractive. It is very filling and rather "heavy", so that it rarely appears on today's Christmas Eve tables, our appetites unfortunately not being what they used to be. But it is worth trying out, since it is both traditional and tasty. The cabbage left over from Christmas Eve may be reheated the next day and served with pork roast. It will be even tastier then.

Pour 2 cups of water over 2 lbs. sauerkraut (if it is very sour, rinse it briefly on a sieve under running water). Cook until tender. Separately, in a small amount of water, cook until tender 2—3 oz. dried mushrooms. Slice the cooked mushrooms into thin strips and add to the cabbage along with the stock. Season the cabbage with a light roux made of 2 tablespoons butter and 1 tablespoon flour, adding also 1 large, finely chopped onion which has been fried in butter to a golden brown. Add salt and pepper to taste and cook a while longer, as the dish should have a thick consistency.

Croquettes: Mash 12 oz. freshly cooked hot potatoes, add 4 oz. ground walnuts, 1 whole egg, a heaped teaspoon of breadcrumbs and a tablespoon of very finely minced green parsley. Salt to taste and mix by hand to a smooth paste. Shape into small croquettes, coat in egg and breadcrumbs, then fry in butter to a golden brown. Arrange the hot croquettes on the cabbage and serve immediately.

Waffles with Poppy Seed

This is a traditional Polish Christmas Eve dessert of seasoned poppy seed decorated with cookies (home-made!). The dish is a fine sight and invariably evokes the admiration of the youngest participants of Christmas Eve supper.

Pour 2 cups of boiling milk over a cup of poppy seed and cook over low heat for 15—20 minutes. Drain thoroughly, then put the poppy seed through a meat grinder three times. Combine the ground poppy seed with 2/3 cup liquid honey, add 1/2 crushed vanilla bean, 4 oz. raisins soaked in rum or cognac and 4 oz. blanched minced almonds. If the poppy-seed paste is too thick, it can be thinned out with a small amount of sweet cream. If the waffles are for adults only, the paste can be perfumed with a wine-glass of good cognac. Cool the poppy-seed paste in the refrigerator. Just before serving, place it in a crystal salad bowl and spike densely with the waffles.

Dough for the Waffles

1) The "lean" version: Knead a thick dough from 5 oz. flour, 5 oz. castor sugar and 1 whole egg. Cut narrow rectangles measuring 1 by 4 inches from the thinly rolled dough and bake in an oven, on a greased metal sheet, to a light golden brown.

2) The rich pastry version: Knead dough from 5 oz. flour, 2 oz. butter, 1 oz. castor sugar and 1 raw egg yolk. The well-kneaded dough should rest in a cool place for 30 minutes. After this time, roll it out thinly and proceed as in the above recipe.

Christmas Eve Compote from Prunes and Figs

Pour cold boiled water over 10 oz. choice prunes (stoned prunes are best), which have been briefly rinsed in lukewarm water, so that the water covers the fruit.

Proceed in the same way with 10 oz. choice figs. It is best to soak the fruit overnight and finish making the compote in the morning.

Add a tablespoon of sugar and a piece of cinnamon to the soaked prunes. Bring to a boil only once in the water in which they have been soaked. The figs, however, are to be cooked for 5 minutes in the water in which they have been soaked, to which has been added a tablespoon of sugar, the juice of a small lemon and a piece of thinly sliced lemon rind.

Combine the separately prepared compotes (remove the cinnamon and lemon rind) and serve at the end of the meal, preferably at room temperature.

Old Polish Christmas Gingerbread

Before we present the Old Polish recipe for Christmas gingerbread, let us say a few words about the Polish gingerbread tradition. The ancient Slavs were already familiar with cake made with honey. But only with the discovery of aromatic spices and leavening ingredients was the hard honey cake, used also in rituals by the Slavs, made into gingerbread.

The Nuremberg and Toruń gingerbreads were the most famous, baked in beautifully carved moulds. The popular katarzynki (honey cakes) from Toruń were known as early as 1640. The Old Polish gingerbread was no worse in quality than the Nuremberg one. The preparation of gingerbread dough was rightly considered to be a real art. It matured slowly and could be stored in its unbaked state for several months. The popularity of gingerbread in Poland is seen in the fact that a pan of gingerbread dough was often part of the dowry of Polish maidens. Very spicy small gingerbread cookies were eaten with vodka, and sweet gingerbread with nuts and raisins was served as a final sweet course. The old Polish proverb says that the best things in Poland used to be liquor from Gdańsk, gingerbread from Toruń, a maiden from Cracow and a shoe from Warsaw. Here is a recipe for gingerbread dough which can be prepared 4 weeks before baking and baked 3—4 days before the holidays, before we begin the most intensive holiday culinary creativity. It can also be baked earlier, but the unbaked dough must mature not less than 2 weeks in a cool place (the lowest shelf in the refrigerator or in a cool cellar, which is better though harder to come by).

Gradually heat 1 lb. real honey, 2 cups sugar, 10 oz. lard (or butter), almost until boiling point. Cool the mixture. To this cool or barely lukewarm mixture add gradually, kneading by hand, 2 lbs. wheat flour, 3 whole eggs, 3 level teaspoons baking soda dissolved in 1/2 cup cold milk, 1/2 teaspoon salt and the following spices: cinnamon, cloves, ginger, cardamon etc. (about 1 1/2—2 1/2 oz. altogether). A handful of crushed nuts may also be added and 3 tablespoons finely chopped candied orange peel.

Knead the dough thoroughly, shape into a ball and place, in a crock covered with a clean linen cloth, in a cool place, so that it can mature slowly.

Divide the matured dough into 2—3 parts and after rolling it out, bake on a metal sheet. Right after baking the cakes are hard, but after 2—3 days they become crumbly and almost melt in your mouth.

Between each layer spread lightly heated, well cooked real plum butter. Other fillings may also be used, e.g. butter, nut and even marzipan fillings. If 3 layers have been baked, one may be covered with jam and the second with a nut filling.

Right after spreading the filling, cover the gingerbread with a piece of clean paper and place a small wooden board or larger books on top evenly.

Old Polish gingerbread retains its freshness for a long time, especially if it is kept in a cool place. It may be covered with chocolate icing and decorated beautifully, but even an undecorated one will doubtless take first place among the traditional Polish Christmas cakes.

Christmas Poppy-Seed Cake

Christmas poppy-seed cake differs from the "everyday" kind not only because the cake layers are thin and the poppy-seed layers thicker, but also because the filling made from poppy seed is prepared with a true Polish generosity that is far from frugal.

We have two kinds of dough to choose from: for yeast cake and for yeast pastry. Both are excellent, although they do not **influence much the flavour of the Christmas** poppy-seed cake. The yeast pastry has the big advantage that its preparation requires very little time, is very easy and does not call for a long mixing process. It may be used, just like the yeast cake, for various rolls and layer cakes.

Yeast Pastry

Cut through with a knife, until well mixed, the following ingredients: 1 lb. wheat flour, 6 oz. butter, 2 oz. yeast thoroughly dissolved in 3 tablespoons cream (slightly sour), 1/2 ground vanilla bean or the grated rind of 1/2 lemon, 2 heaped tablespoons castor sugar, 2 whole eggs and 1 (or 2) egg yolks and 1/3 teaspoon salt.

Knead the dough by hand. It should not be too stiff or shiny. Roll out the dough thinly into a rectangle on a lightly floured board. Spread poppy-seed filling evenly over the dough (leaving a 1 in. wide margin), roll up, transfer carefully to an oblong, buttered pan (the pan may also be lined with buttered aluminium foil) and allow to rise for 1 hour. In order to prevent the dough from splitting, it may be pierced with a pointed wooden skewer. Place the cake directly in a medium hot oven for 45—50 minutes.

Yeast Cake

This is prepared from 12 oz. wheat flour, 6 oz. castor sugar, 6 oz. butter, 2 whole eggs (or 1 egg and 2 egg yolks), 1/2 cup milk, 1 1/2 oz. yeast and a pinch of salt. Cream the butter with the sugar and when well blended, add gradually the following ingredients: the eggs, salt and the yeast dissolved in lukewarm milk. Finally add the flour and knead the dough well by hand. After kneading, the dough should be allowed to rise (covered with a cloth) for not less than an hour. After this, roll out the dough thinly on a floured board, shaping it into a rectangle, cover with egg white (so that the filling does not separate from the cake) and spread filling evenly. Roll the cake up tightly, pressing well on the ends, not rolling them under.

The poppy-seed cake thus prepared should rise before baking in a buttered pan. The baking time is 45—50 minutes.

After baking and cooling, the cake (in both versions) may be covered with lemon icing and, before the icing sets, sprinkled with finely chopped, lightly browned almonds.

Poppy-Seed Filling

Pour 1 3/4 pints boiling milk over 1 lb. poppy seed which has been washed. Cook (the milk should barely simmer) over low heat for 30 minutes. Drain the poppy seed on a sieve and put through a meat grinder (use the finest sieve) 3—4 times.

In a cast-iron pot melt 6 oz. butter, 3/4 cup honey, add a finely ground vanilla bean, 4 oz. not too finely ground almonds (or other nuts), 6 oz. raisins and 1/2 cup finely chopped candied orange peel. Now add the poppy seed and fry together with the above ingredients for 15 minutes (mixing often to avoid burning). Cool the mixture slightly and add 3—4 egg yolks, well beaten with a cup of sugar. Add the remaining egg whites, beaten stiffly. The flavour will be even more elegant if a brandy-glass of good rum or cognac is added. The filling is ready. Spread it on the cake while still lukewarm.

The preparation of this exquisite filling is costly and takes a lot of effort, but then Christmas is celebrated only once a year.

The carnival was a colourful, sometimes too merry epilogue to Christmas holidays. In the olden days it was a period of particularly active socializing in Poland. During the carnival, entertainment included hunting, weddings along with feasts and balls that lasted several days, carnival parties, masquerades and the famous Old Polish *kuligs* (sleigh-rides).

These uproarious parties, often accompanied by gluttony and drinking, shocked the clerical and secular moralists. The priest Jakub Wujek (1541—97), the excellent translator of the Bible into Polish, said that carnivals were "invented by the devil!"

"We make a greater profit for the devil, making merry without restraint for three days, than for the Lord when we fast unwillingly for forty days," adds Grzegorz from Żarnowiec (1528—1601). Mikołaj Rej, on the other hand, disapproved of masquerades: "On a carnival Sunday whoever does not go mad..., does not change his face, does not think up a mask and dress so that he resembles the devil, supposedly does not carry out his Christian duty."

Kuligs were very popular among the gentry. The closest neighbours arranged to set out on several sleighs and on horseback, visiting other homes. The surprised host had to receive the unexpected guests with everything that he had in his pantry and cellar, after which he joined the *kulig*, which set out for the next house. At individual stopovers there was not only feasting, but dancing as well, accompanied by musicians picked up by chance, unless the party set out with their own musicians. The women, wrapped in furs, went on the sleighs, the men on horseback. Servants accompanied the *kulig* on horseback, by night lighting the way with torches. The Old Polish *kulig* by night presented an unusually colourful and also noisy picture, as the somewhat intoxicated men often fired shots in the air, sometimes in order to drive away the packs of wolves, but more often simply for the fun of it.

The beautiful image of a Polish *kulig* was revived by Stefan Żeromski (1864—1925) in his famous novel *Popioły* (Ashes), also made into a film.

There were no special carnival delicacies. On feasts and balls more elegant dishes were served, not omitting such genuinely Polish dishes as *bigos*. Only among cakes there were carnival *faworki* (fried strips of pastry dusted with icing sugar) and *pączki* (doughnuts). During the reign of Augustus III, Father Jędrzej Kitowicz, noted in his *Description of Customs during the Reign of Augustus III* that Polish doughnuts could compete with the famous Viennese doughnuts: "A doughnut of long ago could blacken the eye when hitting it, today a doughnut is so light that if squeezed in the hand, it stretches out once again and swells like a sponge to its former volume and the wind would blow it off a platter."

Indeed, Polish doughnuts, light, aromatic and delicate, became very popular. Even today the inhabitants of Warsaw consume over two million confectionery *pączki* on the last Thursday of carnival, not to mention those which are fried in many homes according to old family recipes.

Not only the gentry, but the city and village common folk enjoyed themselves as well during carnival. These parties were less noisy, but there was no lack of food or drink. Dances and masquerades were held. Naturally, carnival was an occasion most of all for young people to have their fling. Many practical jokes were played which went by unpunished, provided they were not carried too far. In wealthy burgher homes carnival parties were no worse than in a nobleman's home as far as the splendour of dishes, music and dance was concerned, although it must be emphasized that they usually took place without the excesses of the gentry. Apprentices enjoyed themselves the most, in their own company. The daughters of the master were also invited to such parties. The one who invited the lady had to see to it that she had a good time. If she did not have a partner for each dance, the young man had to pay a fine. The company not only ate, drank and danced, but also sang songs, sometimes with quite frivolous lyrics.

The above mentioned Father Jędrzej Kitowicz describes a carnival party of Cracow stall-holders — women known for their unrestrained tongues and fiery temperaments. The party, given on the Cracow market square, had long traditions full of humour and vigour and worth recalling. This party, called a *comber*, used to take place on the last Thursday of carnival. On this day "the stall-holders had their wish, hired musicians, brought over various kinds of food and drink and in the middle of the market square, on the street, they danced, even in the greatest mud; they drew into their dance whatever man they could catch. The lean and hungry allowed themselves to be caught for the sake of the food and drink; and if a distinguished person came by who was unaware of the custom, he usually preferred to pay his way out rather than jump about in the mud and in the company of these women." This interesting *comber* was therefore a kind of democratic festivity of the townsfolk and only the "distinguished" refused to take part.

In the villages the young farmhands went around with a wooden cock on a cart, obtaining cheese, butter, bacon, *kiełbasa* and eggs from the girls and even the more matronly women. In the end they organized a merry feast from the collected food, along with drinks. This going around the village with the cock was most likely an echo of some very old folk pagan rite.

Carnival came to an end and on Ash Wednesday the long reign of *żur* (a kind of sour soup) and herring began.

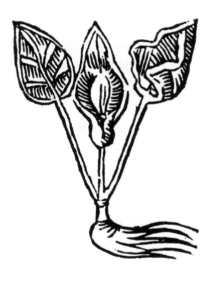

Easter

Easter, the most important

Christian holiday, became the greatest culinary holiday in older Poland. When we read descriptions of Old Polish Easter feasts — not the ones given by the magnates in their manors, but the more modest ones in noblemen's and burgher homes and even in peasant cottages — we get the impression that the religious, or spiritual side of this holiday was pushed into the background in favour of the earthly pleasures of the palate.

Lent, which preceded Easter, was the overture to the Easter feasts. In the beginning, Lent was observed very strictly, even at the royal court, but this did not last very long. Only the poor townsfolk and peasants fasted like true Catholics, for religious as well as material reasons. They ate *żur*, kashas, cabbage, herring and later potatoes flavoured only with oil.

The Mazurians fasted in the most exemplary fashion. It was said that "a Mazurian would sooner kill a man, than break fast during Lent". They did not use butter, nor even milk during Lent.

At the palaces of the magnates and in wealthy monasteries fasting was carried out in a specific way. Various tastily seasoned dishes were served and not in fasting quantities at all. Therefore, depending on the situation, the idea of Lent could be interpreted in various ways, especially as alcoholic beverages were not forbidden.

On Good Friday the young nobles and burghers organized a "funeral of *żur* and herring". A clay pot with *żur* was shattered and a herring was hung on a branch as punishment "that for six weeks it had ruled over meat, starving human stomachs with its meagre nourishment". On Easter Saturday, in towns as well as in villages, eggs and salt were carried to church, where they were blessed and then placed on the holiday table. Easter in Polish folk cooking was much more modest than in the homes of the gentry, but it had stronger ties with the old customs and rituals. Among the relics of these still pagan beliefs are *pisanki* i.e. hard-boiled eggs, coloured and artistically decorated by village women. The custom of colouring eggs for Easter is still observed. The Easter eggs of old were often true works of folk art; today's Easter eggs usually cannot compare as far as artistic skill and decorative detail are concerned. The egg being an ancient symbol of life, it reigned on Easter tables, since Easter is at the same time a holiday of nature's awakening to life. Easter eggs were very often painted red; according to old Slavic beliefs, they had magical properties and were said to be effective particularly in matters of the heart.

In eastern Poland on Good Friday the village women presented eggs to the priest, especially painted eggs. The Frenchman Guillaume de Beauplan, military engineer, architect and excellent cartographer who visited Poland during the reign of Sigismund III Vasa and Ladislaus IV (in the years 1630—48), described this custom, stating that within two hours the priest collected up to 5,000 eggs. Thanking the pious offerers, he kissed the girls and younger women and gave his hand to be kissed to the older women.

On the magnates' and noblemen's estates the magnificently laid Easter table was blessed by a parish-priest or chaplain. During Holy Week the greatest activity took place in the kitchen, from which drifted delicious smells of food being prepared for the holiday. They aroused the appetite of fasting household members who were waiting impatiently for Easter, which meant the end of Lent and the beginning of the Easter culinary battle.

The delicacies blessed by the priest were placed on a big table in the dining-room. They consisted of hams, *kiełbasas*, brawn, fish in aspic, a pig baked whole and Easter cakes: *mazureks*, layer cakes and the famous Old Polish *babas*. Of course, vodkas, meads, beer and wine were not forgotten. An Easter lamb formed from butter or sugar was placed in the middle. The whole table, full of colour and tempting with delicious smells, was decorated with green myrtle branches and coloured eggs.

These Easter tables were modest sometimes and stunningly rich at other times, all of which depended on the wealth of the house.

For example, the apprentices in towns, hungry after a long lasting and strictly observed Lent, awaited the relatively modest meal at their master's with great longing. This can be seen in the surviving verses of songs sung by apprentices on Palm Sunday. In these passages we sense not only a religious mood, but a sharpened impatient and young appetite. Here are two samples of these somewhat audacious, but charmingly honest songs:

> *Layer cakes*
> *And stuffed kiełbasas are good*
> *Let me, Christ, taste this*
> *Let me see these Easter delicacies*

> *I shall praise you that you are good, Lord,*
> *When I eat some ham for breakfast.*

Even the most modest Easter feast was begun with the sharing of a blessed hard-boiled egg, which was accompanied by an exchange of greetings. Right after this, everyone sat down to the table, which was a prototype of today's cold buffet in its arrangement of dishes.

The Easter cakes — *babas* and *mazureks* — deserve special mention. Layer cakes are a relatively late acquisition and the fashion for them came doubtless from Italy, thanks to Queen Bona.

Babas and *mazureks* are characteristic of Old Polish cooking as they are genuinely Polish delicacies.

The baking of Easter *babas* was an exciting event and could be called a kind of magic art. The cook, the lady of the house and all the women of the household locked themselves in the kitchen. Men were forbidden to enter. The whitest wheat flour was sifted through a fine sieve, hundreds (!) of egg yolks were beaten with sugar in bowls, saffron was dissolved in vodka (it not only coloured the cake beautifully, but gave it a spicy aroma as well), almonds were ground, raisins were sorted, fragrant vanilla was ground in mortars and yeast was dissolved. The dough was put into *baba* moulds and covered with linen cloths, since a "cold" *baba* did not grow and could not be baked thoroughly. Therefore, the kitchen windows and doors were made airtight to avoid draughts. The risen *babas* were carefully placed in the baking oven. Finally, when they were taken out of the hot oven on a wooden spade, frequently there were dramatic cries and tears: a *baba* that was too brown or had collapsed meant loss of face. When the *babas* were taken out, they were carefully placed on an eiderdown so that they would not be crushed when cooling. Everyone spoke in whispers since any noise could also harm the delicate cake. The cooked *babas* were beautifully and liberally iced. The most famous and delicate were the "feather" and "muslin" *babas*.

The origin of *mazureks* has not been sufficiently explained yet. It is possible that they were influenced by the sweet cuisine of the Turks. *Mazureks* are flat cakes, usually on a pastry or on a wafer, covered with a paste of nuts, almonds, cheese, or nuts with raisins etc., colourfully iced and decorated with jam and nuts and raisins. Good cooks often had several recipes for *mazureks*.

Let the description of an Easter reception at Prince Sapieha's palace in Dereczyn give us a picture of an Easter of the magnates. It took place during the reign of King Ladislaus IV:

"There were four gigantic boars, that is as many as there are seasons; each boar had in it pork, *alias* ham, *kiełbasas* and piglets. The head cook showed the most wonderful skill in the roasting of these boars whole. Then there were twelve stags, also roasted whole, with the golden horns to be admired, stuffed with various game, *alias* hares, black grouse, bustards and grouse. These stags stood for the twelve months. Around them there were lengthy cakes, as many as there are weeks in a year, that is fifty-two, wonderful whole cakes, *mazurek*, *pierogi* from Samogitia and everything was covered with nuts and raisins. Behind this there were 365 *babas*, that is as many as there are days in a year. Each one was adorned with inscriptions and ornaments, so that more than one person only read without eating. As for drinking: there were four bowls, to represent the four seasons, filled with wine dating from the reign of King Stephen [Báthory]. Then there were 12 silver jars of wine from the reign of King Sigismund, representing the 12 months. There were 52 silver barrels representing the 52 weeks and filled with wine from Cyprus, Spain and Italy. Then there were 365 demijohns with Hungarian wine, *alias* as many as there are days in a year. And for the royal servants there were 8,700 quarts of mead, as many as there are hours in a year."

Many such parties were given among the magnates and the above was by no means the most magnificent one.

These grand luxuries of the magnates used up huge fortunes and were ruinous for the health. Therefore it is no wonder that our more sensible ancestors called the Old Polish cooking of the magnates "an impediment of the noble substance".

Someone who reprimanded culinary luxury intended to impress only, was the great writer Mikołaj Rej, who lived during the reign of King Sigismund Augustus, himself a lover of pomp and luxury.

The mother of this monarch, wife of Sigismund the Old, the Italian princess Bona Sforza, introduced Italian customs to the royal court. Cracow was full of Italians, who occupied various, always profitable, posts. This contact of two cultures on a high level was beneficial in many instances, especially in the fields of art, architecture, literature and music. Italian influence began to make itself known in Polish cooking as well, though with some impediments. The Italians were surprised to see how much meat Poles consumed every day. Poles, on the other hand, made fun of the

Italians' love for vegetables, which in their opinion was exaggerated. The papal nuncio, Ruggieri, while on a visit to Poland in 1565, stated that "one Pole will eat as much meat as five Italians", and Poles answered that "an Italian feeds on lettuce, a Pole becomes thin on it".* This really exaggerated fondness for meat, which is not good for the health, has survived to this day. The Easter table with its delicacies is an example of this today as well as long ago.

But let us return to Mikołaj Rej. In his work entitled *The Life of an Honest Man*, written in a picturesque and straightforward style, he praises the simple peasant delicacies, writing about them almost with tenderness and also giving many excellent recipes. But he reprimands elaborate dishes, not mincing his words to do so. Here are a few quotations: "Only observe these strange dishes and these indecent inventions of today's world... On one dish you have a gilded lamb, on another a lion, on a third a lady... and the dish in the middle represents the devil; it is rancid and slimy, and would be far better and tastier if it were placed warm on the platter straight from the enamelled pot... And so from these strange inventions... only indecent waste, then a variety of ulcers and numerous harmful cases."

We admit that the wise Mikołaj Rej was right, but it seems that he himself, even though he wrote so sensibly, was not one who could boast of the virtue of moderation in food and drink. And even today we rarely listen to our common sense, not only when preparing the traditional Easter delicacies.

Cold meats will be ready-made and bought in a shop, of course. Polish hams and *kiełbasas* are after all deservedly popular today all over the world.

But Easter cakes will be home-baked, according to the old recipes preserved in the notes of our grandmothers and great grandmothers.

Let us begin with the Easter *babas*.

* It was said that a certain nobleman, having set out to Italy in spring for a longer stay, returned to Poland in early autumn, as he was afraid that since he had been given so much lettuce in summer, in winter he would be given hay.

Muslin Baba

Break 24 egg yolks into an enamelled dish, adding 12 oz. sugar. Place dish with egg yolks into a larger dish with hot water and beat with an egg-beater until thick and light in colour. Then add yeast (crumble 2 oz. yeast in 1/2 cup lukewarm milk, add 1 tablespoon flour and 1 teaspoon sugar, mix and wait until it rises, then add the yeast to the beaten egg yolks), 1 tablespoon vanilla ground to a powder and 10 oz. sifted and lightly warmed wheat flour. Beat the dough for 30 minutes, then add 4 oz. melted lukewarm butter and beat again for 30 minutes. When the dough doubles in bulk (in a warm place), transfer it to a buttered, lightly warmed baba pan. When the dough rises to the edges in the pan, place it in a well-heated oven, taking care to avoid any sudden jolts. In a medium-hot oven the baking time is 60—70 minutes.

The muslin baba, when successfully baked, is a cake of the highest rank.

Fluffy Baba

This is much cheaper and requires less work, but also makes a high class cake. Scald 10 oz. wheat flour with boiling milk and mix very well until all lumps are gone. Cover and cool. Next, add 2 1/2 oz. yeast, mix and allow it to rise, covered.

Beat 10 egg yolks with 6 oz. castor sugar to a fluffy cream. Add the beaten egg yolks and 10 oz. flour more to the yeast and knead very thoroughly, so that the dough does not stick to the bowl or hand. Then add 6 oz. melted butter, a small brandy glass of rum and a pinch of salt. Knead the dough thoroughly by hand once more and add 8 oz. raisins in the end.

Place the dough in a buttered pan. Let it rise, covered, and when it fills the pan almost completely, bake in a well heated oven (50—55 minutes).

Having taken the hot baba out of the pan, sprinkle liberally with castor sugar, or cover with white icing when cooled.

Saffron Baba

This is an exquisite cake with a truly Old Polish note, much more attractive than the banal cakes and cookies from a confectioner's. When carefully prepared and baked just right, it is the pride of an Easter table in the Polish style.

To 10 oz. flour add 3/4 pint lukewarm milk and mix with 3 oz. yeast. Leave this in a warm place for an hour, covered with a cloth, until it grows nicely. Then add the following ingredients, which have been beaten with 6 oz. sugar: 8 egg yolks and 4 egg whites, the rind of 1 small lemon, which has been soaked (for 3 hours) in a brandy-glass of spirit, a pinch of saffron (well-sieved), mix thoroughly with the yeast, add 30 oz. flour, a small teaspoon of salt and knead the dough by hand for 30 minutes. Into the kneaded dough pour 6 oz. lukewarm, melted butter, add 4 oz. raisins and 1 oz. thin candied orange peel. Knead the dough by hand until it does not stick to your hand or to the bowl. Now place it in a buttered pan; allow the dough to rise and when it fills the pan, place the baba in a well heated oven. The baking time is a little over 60 minutes. Test with a thin wooden skewer. If it comes out clean, the cake is done. Sprinkle the warm baba with castor sugar or cover with icing.

Mazureks are baked on baking sheets. They should be rectangular and the size of a sheet of typewriter paper. Mazureks are baked in round cake-pans only when we make no cakes, otherwise both of these completely different types of cake unnecessarily become similar in shape. Mazureks should not be high, and so the mazurek dough is placed on the baking sheet finger-thick.

Foamy Nut Mazurek

In a bowl cream until fluffy 3 raw egg yolks with 10 oz. castor sugar, adding 5 oz. butter in small portions while creaming. To this thoroughly blended butter and egg yolk mixture add 5 oz. wheat flour and 10 oz. ground walnuts and, joining these ingredients, knead into a smooth dough.

Line the mazurek baking-sheet with wafers (if possible, use wafers the size of typewriter paper), place the dough evenly on the wafers and smooth out its surface with a knife.

Beat 3 egg yolks until stiff, adding 3 oz. castor sugar while beating. Cover the dough evenly with the beaten egg whites and arrange halves of shelled nuts, not too close to each other, at the sides of the surface.

Bake the mazurek in a medium-hot oven, as it should not brown too much. Bake two days before the holidays, so that it becomes crumbly.

Old Polish Royal Mazurek

In a bowl cream 14 oz. of the finest butter until fluffy. Add 5 oz. castor sugar, 5 oz. blanched almonds finely chopped (not ground!) a little lemon rind, 15 oz. wheat flour, 4 hard-boiled and sieved egg yolks, 1 raw egg yolk and a pinch of salt.

Knead these ingredients into a smooth dough, which should "rest" in a cool place for at least an hour.

Roll out 2/3 of the dough until finger-thick and with it line a buttered baking-sheet lightly dusted with flour. Roll out the remaining dough into thin strips that are pencil-thick and arrange into a lattice-work pattern on the dough. Coat the whole mazurek (with the aid of a feather or soft flat brush) with a raw egg yolk and bake in a well heated oven to a light golden colour.

When the mazurek cools completely, place thoroughly drained fruit from preserves into the open spaces of the lattice-work. The whole may be covered with icing.

Date Mazurek

Beat 6—7 egg whites until stiff, adding 20 oz. castor sugar in tablespoonfuls while beating. The egg whites should be so stiff and shiny that they can be cut with a knife.

This takes 30 minutes by hand in a bowl (10 minutes with an electric beater at high speed). After this, add 10 oz. thinly sliced dates (without pits!), 10 oz. finely chopped blanched almonds and 10 oz. grated semi-sweet chocolate, without beating. After mixing these ingredients lightly, place the mazurek paste finger-thick on wafers and bake in a moderately hot oven, so that the mazureks dry rather than bake.

After the baking and thorough cooling, trim the edges with a sharp knife, then cover with an icing made of sugar and water with pineapple essence or from sugar blended with orange liqueur (or orange vodka).

From these proportions we get two mazureks.

Nut Mazurek from Egg Whites

When baking Easter cakes, often there are leftover egg whites which we do not know what to do with. These egg whites can be used for making an exquisite mazurek. Beat 10—11 egg whites with 10 oz. castor sugar until very stiff. Combine gently with 10 oz. ground nuts (or unskinned almonds), or with a mixture of ground almonds, walnuts and hazelnuts with 2 tablespoons sponge-cake put through a sieve and a finely ground vanilla bean. Place the paste on a buttered baking-sheet dusted with flour and bake in a not too hot oven for 3 5—40 minutes.

Two exquisite mazureks come out of these proportions, enabling us to get rid of the leftover egg whites.

Cover the completely cooled mazureks with coffee icing, decorating them with lightly browned almond halves or with a colourful folk-style Easter egg.

The decoration of the Easter table is supplemented by one or more layer-cakes. As far as layer-cakes are concerned, the Polish cuisine can compete with the Austrian cuisine, from which we have adopted many excellent recipes, adding to them the "inspired" authentically Polish recipes. Layer-cakes were especially popular on the Polish territories that went to Austria after the partitions of Poland (carried out by Prussia, Russia and Austria in the years 1772, 1793 and 1795, with Austria taking part only in the first and third partitions). These were the peak years of Austria's political power and of the glorious rise of the Austrian cuisine, which drew many of its attractions from the kitchens of its subject nations.

Cracow Pastry Layer-Cake

This is an exquisite "dry" layer-cake which gets better the longer it is kept. Thus, it can be baked 3—4 days before the holidays, so that it matures and becomes as crumbly as happiness. The great advantage of this cake is also that it is not filled with the high-calorie and rich butter filling.

Knead a pastry dough quickly from 10 oz. butter, 10 oz. flour, 5 oz. ground (blanched) almonds, 4 hard-boiled egg yolks, 5 oz. castor sugar and 1/2 vanilla bean ground to a powder and sifted through a sieve. Bake 4—5 thin round layers in a baking pan in turns. The layers should not be browned too much, but should be lightly golden.

To make the filling between the layers: beat 4 egg whites with 4 oz. castor sugar until stiff. Add 8 oz. apricot jam put through a sieve. The marmalade (jam) has to be of the finest quality. After adding the jam, cream the paste until fluffy.

Spread the filling thinly between the layers

which form the cake. All of the filling can be used this way and the cake can be covered with icing made from 5 oz. castor sugar, 5 oz. sieved apricot jam and 1 tablespoon freshly squeezed lemon juice. Before the icing sets, the cake can be decorated with rosettes made from almond halves.

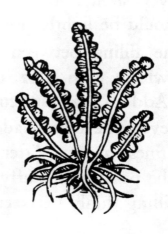

Polish Chocolate Layer-Cake

Cream 12 egg yolks with 8 oz. castor sugar until fluffy and, while still creaming, add 10 oz. powdered chocolate (not cocoa!), 10 oz. almonds ground with the skins and mix in lightly 12 stiffly beaten egg whites. Place in a buttered cake-pan lightly dusted with flour. Bake for 1 hour.

Next day, slice the cake into two layers of equal thickness and fill with the following almond paste: cook 10 oz. sugar and 1 cup water until a thick syrup forms. Pour 10 oz. ground almonds (blanched!) into the syrup while cooking and bring to the boil only once. Place the paste in a bowl and cream with a wooden pestle until pale in colour, adding 3 tablespoons lemon juice and 1/2 vanilla bean, very finely ground and sieved. Spread between the layers while still warm.

The cake is covered with chocolate icing made from 6 oz. semi-sweet, ground and warmed chocolate with 1 1/2 oz. butter, 4 oz. sugar and half a cup of sweet cream.

Nut-Almond Cake
(without flour or filling)

This is one of the most original cakes known in Polish cookery. The fact that it has no filling is to its advantage, since thanks to this, the nut and almond aromas can develop fully, mingling in a truly exquisite way. This cake consists of two layers of different colour and flavour, one placed on top of the other and baked together.

First, prepare the nut dough: cream 10 egg yolks with 10 oz. castor sugar until fluffy, at the same time adding 1 heaped tablespoon sifted cocoa (best quality), mixed with a little milk. Next, add 10 oz. ground walnuts and 1 vanilla bean ground to a powder. Spread this paste evenly on the bottom of a large cake-pan, buttered and dusted with potato flour.

Immediately prepare the second, almond dough: Beat 10 egg whites until very stiff, gradually adding 10 oz. sifted castor sugar.

Add the juice of 1/2 lemon and 1 vanilla bean ground to a powder, 3 tablespoons ground sponge-cake put through a large sieve, and 10 oz. ground almonds (blanched). After mixing thoroughly, place the dough on the walnut dough making it higher in the center of the pan, since the cake tends to collapse somewhat during baking.

Place the pan in a medium-hot oven for 50-55 minutes.

The next day cover the cake (the top and sides) with a not too thin layer of warm orange marmalade. When this sets, coat with chocolate icing, though in our opinion coffee icing is a better alternative.

Easter breakfast at which the blessed delicacies were eaten, was begun quite early, at noon or somewhat later. In some homes the more impatient men attacked the holiday table on Easter Saturday directly after the Resurrection Service, which meant the end of Lent fasting. But usually these were only the preludes to the Sunday culinary battle.

The delicacies consisted only of cold dishes, with a variety of flavours and aromas.

The only hot dish was red borsch, made of soured beet juice. It differed from the Christmas Eve borsch in that it was cooked with a concentrated meat stock, often with the stock from cooked ham. Instead of *uszka* (a kind of ravioli), quarters of hard-boiled eggs or sliced *kiełbasa* were placed in the borsch. However, we believe that for dietetic reasons and in view of the abundance of other rich dishes, it will be better if, contrary to tradition, we serve the leaner Christmas Eve borsch. The final course was hot *bigos*, but we shall devote more attention to this famous Old Polish dish in a while.

Some of the Easter dishes were once connected with various folk beliefs, not taken too seriously of course. We learn from Mikołaj Rej that *kiełbasa*, for example, protected against snake-bite, horseradish against fleas and roast hazel grouse against... prison.

To those who like to fast well, we shall now serve a Christmas Eve or Good Friday lunch consisting of the two traditional fasting dishes: *żur* (a kind of sour soup) and herring Polish style.

Żur

This is a lightly sour, refreshing soup made from the so-called white borsch, i.e. from soured rye flour
The soured juice for the żur should be prepared earlier, as it can be stored for up to two weeks in tightly corked bottles in a cool place. It is made in the following way:
Scald 2 cups whole-rye flour with boiling water, pouring in enough to get a thin dough. When it cools, add 1 3/4 pints lukewarm water and place a piece of wholemeal bread crust in this. Pour into a glass jar, tie with gauze and leave in a warm place. After three days the white borsch is ready to use.

Lent Żur

Cook 1 3/4 pints vegetable stock (celeriac and parsley root, carrots, leeks, onion) with dried mushrooms and add 3/4 pint white borsch to the hot stock. Do not strain, as

the soup should be slightly thick. If the żur
is not sour enough, add some more white
borsch. Add a crushed garlic clove to the
boiling soup, along with 4 potatoes cut into
cubes. When the potatoes are soft, salt to
taste. The potatoes can also be served
separately, seasoned with onion fried in
oil.

Żur with Kiełbasa

This is made like the Lent żur, with the one
difference that it is cooked with kiełbasa,
which is taken out before serving, thinly
sliced and returned to the soup. 2 oz. lean
bacon can also be used. It is chopped into
very small cubes and fried in a frying pan,
then added to the żur. If the żur is cooked
with kiełbasa, garlic need not be added, but
garlic does give it much more character. The
potatoes can be cooked either in the
soup (cut into cubes), or served separately,
seasoned with pork fat and cracklings (fried
onion can also be added).

Herrings Polish Style

Soak 4 fine salt milter-herrings in cold water for 24 hours changing the water several times while soaking.

Remove the skin carefully from the soaked herrings, remove the milt, cut off the tail and head, divide into fillets and remove the bones.

Arrange the fillets in layers in a glass jar. Between the layers place very thin slices of onion (2 onions), 10 grains of pepper, 6 grains of pimento (allspice), one bay leaf broken into parts and 5 slices of lemon (without rind or pits).

Combine 1/2 pint sweet cream with the juice of 3 large lemons and the herring milt that has been put through a wire-sieve. Do not salt the sauce, but add 1/2 teaspoon castor sugar.

Pour the sauce over the fillets in the jar (shake the jar slightly to spread the sauce evenly) and close securely with paper. Place the covered jar in a cool place. After

24 hours, the herrings are matured and make an excellent Lent dinner dish.

Baked potatoes are served with herrings Polish style. Peel the potatoes, cover lightly with oil, dust with salt and caraway seed, then bake in oven.

In the treasury of Old Polish culinary recipes *bigos* is one of the most precious jewels. Its traditions go back far into the past and the future predicts further long-lasting popularity for this dish.

In older days *bigos*, stored in wooden casks or great stoneware pots, was a necessary component of a well-equipped pantry. Reheating the *bigos* many times only adds to the flavour and aroma. Thus an unexpected guest could be served *bigos*, or it was eaten on hunting expeditions, when it was heated in a kettle hung over an open fire. A cask of *bigos* was taken "for the road", since it was part of the classical Old Polish traveling food supply. It was also served during carnival, at Easter feasts and on many other occasions. The tastiest *bigos* was made during Christmas and Easter, as there was a great variety of meat and game on hand, and these make up the essence of *bigos*.

We find many good words about this dish in Old Polish literature. But the most beautiful literary monument to *bigos* is Adam Mickiewicz's praise, found in that masterpiece of Polish literature, *Pan Tadeusz*:

> The bigos is being cooked. No words can tell
> The wonder of its colour, taste and smell.
> Mere words and rhymes are jingling sounds, whose sense
> No city stomach really comprehends.
> For Lithuanian food and song you ought
> To have good health and country life and sport.
> But bigos e'en without such sauce is good,
> Of vegetables curiously brewed.
> The basis of it is sliced sauerkraut,
> Which, as they say, just walks into the mouth;
> Enclosed within a cauldron, its moist breast
> Lies on the choisest meat in slices pressed.
> There it is parboiled till the heat draws out
> The living juices from the cauldron's spout,
> And all the air is fragrant with the smell.
> 'Twas ready now.*

*Cf. p. 98

Bigos

Bigos is a composition not only complex, but also with a great many variants. In each Old Polish kitchen it was made in a different way, in accordance with home traditions. Thus, there was hunting bigos, Lithuanian bigos, rascal's bigos and others, made with sauerkraut, with sauerkraut and fresh cabbage and with fresh cabbage only. Take 3 lbs. sauerkraut of fresh cabbage for 2 lbs. various meats (kiełbasa or ham should prevail). Equal parts of sauerkraut and fresh cabbage may also be taken. Some, however, take 3 lbs. assorted meats for 2 lbs. cabbage (sour or fresh) and no one has said anything against these generous Old Polish proportions, especially since this practice appears to be rare today.

The assorted meats should consist of the following, cut into cubes: pork roast, roast beef, joint of pork cooked in vegetables, a piece of roast duck and sliced kiełbasa (better: various kinds of sausages if possible, along with lean cooked ham cut into cubes). The addition of roast game raises the flavour of bigos considerably, but without game it will be just as excellent. Sauces from roast meats are also added to the bigos.

The sauerkraut can be chopped and fresh cabbage can be thinly sliced and scalded with boiling water before cooking. Cook the cabbage over low heat in a small amount of water (better: in the stock from cooked kiełbasa). If only fresh cabbage is used, add 1 1/2 lbs. sour apples, peeled and finely chopped, towards the end of cooking. Apples are also added to sauerkraut, but in a smaller amount (4 large sour apples). Separately, cook at least 2 oz. dried mushrooms. Slice the cooked mushrooms thinly and add to the cabbage and heat along with the stock.

Now add 2 large, finely chopped onions lightly browned in lard or butter. If a richer bigos is preferred, fry the onions in 2—4 oz. lard. While the bigos is simmering, add 20 prunes (stoned), cut into strips. The prunes may be substituted by 1 — 2 tablespoons well fried plum butter.

Season the bigos with salt, pepper and, if desired, with a little sugar. It should be sharp in taste. Finally, add 1/2 — 2/3 cup dry red wine or madeira. After adding all the ingredients, cook the bigos over low heat for 40 minutes (careful: stir often, as it tends to burn). Next day, reheat the bigos. It is tastiest and "mature" after the third reheating.

Some add a roux of flour lightly browned in fat, which makes the bigos thicker. But if the bigos is well cooked, in our opinion, this addition is unnecessary.

The bigos may also be seasoned with a tablespoon of thick tomato paste. Old Polish cuisine did not make use of this because it was not known then. But we strongly recommend the addition of tomato paste. Cook the bigos in an enamelled or cast-iron enamelled pot, but never in an aluminium one.

Serve it very hot. Whole-wheat (or white) bread is served separately, along with a glass of chilled vodka (Wyborowa, Rye or Żubrówka), which improves digestion.

The skill of making a genuinely Polish bigos is acquired through practice. It should be made with concentration, with frequent tasting in order to achieve the full harmony of artfully measured out ingredients. Haste and a distracted mind are particularly dangerous. Such an unsuccessful bigos is described in the biting epigram by Wacław Potocki:

> *Wanting to season her bigos in haste,*
> *A maiden goes to the cupboard to add vinegar for taste.*
> *There among the bottles stood ink, as it was frosty outside*
> *Having poured it in she gives me the new dish, with pride.*
> *I try it: a dog wouldn't eat it; and I think in some wrath:*
> *I've never seen bigos in mourning; by my troth!*

Stuffed Roast Pig

This magnificent creation, which once decorated most Polish Easter tables, now is a very costly and rare, truly Old Polish delicacy. Since the Easter meal is often especially festive, for example being a wedding reception at the same time, perhaps it is worth considering whether or not to serve roast pig. One way or the other, just reading about this recipe is a pleasure, although a somewhat nostalgic one.

5—6 week old suckling pigs are the tastiest. After killing the pig and scalding it with boiling water, shave off the bristles very thoroughly with a very sharp knife. Just to be sure, the shaven pig may be singed over a spirit flame (particularly the ears). After shaving the pig, cover it with very cold water for one hour, then draw, setting aside the lungs, liver and heart. Then wash the pig in cold water, dry with a clean linen cloth and salt one hour before roasting. After this time, stuff with the chosen farce,

arrange on a large oven-pan with the back
side up and the legs tucked under and roast
in a well-heated oven. During roasting, the
pig is often basted with a feather dipped
alternately in beer and in melted butter.
This makes the pig brown nicely and evenly
to an orange-brown colour and the skin
becomes deliciously crisp.

Farce No. 1.

Simmer in butter the liver, lungs and heart
of the pig with 20 oz. boned veal and with
a finely chopped onion and vegetables
(parsley and celeriac root, 1 carrot). Remove
the liver earlier, as soon as it becomes tender. Grind the lungs, liver and meat in a
meat grinder. Cook 12 oz. pork fat and cut
into small cubes when cooled. Soak 2 white
rolls (grate the crust off) in milk and squeeze
out well. Mix the ground meats, pork fat
and rolls thoroughly with 2 raw eggs and
the sauce in which the meat has simmered.
Salt to taste and season with ground nutmeg
and freshly ground pepper.

Farce No. 2

This is a typical Old Polish farce, made from kasha. Mix 2 cups not too fine Cracow kasha with 1 raw egg. Roasted buckwheat may also be used, which does not need the egg. Pour 1 1/3 pint salted boiling water over the kasha, cook, and, when thickened, add 2 oz. lard or butter and a teaspoon of finely minced dill (the latter is not necessary, especially in winter). Next, roast the kasha in an oven for 35 minutes. Pour the roasted kasha into a bowl and cool. Grind the liver and lungs and add to the kasha along with 2 whole eggs and 4 oz. cooked diced pork fat. Salt to taste, season with pepper, nutmeg and a pinch of marjoram. 1/2 cup concentrated broth (bouillon) may also be added to the kasha. Mix the farce well and stuff the pig with it.

Farce No. 3

This farce, with raisins and almonds, also has a characteristic Polish note and it is perhaps for this reason that it is particularly good for stuffing an Easter pig, as it contrasts in flavour with other meats.

Simmer the liver and lungs in 1 oz. butter, adding some water, until the meat browns slightly. Next, grind in a meat grinder along with 3 white rolls that have been soaked in milk and squeezed out well.

Cream 3 oz. butter until light and fluffy, adding 3 raw egg yolks while beating; add the ground meat with rolls, salt to taste, add 1 teaspoon sugar, season scantily with pepper and a pinch of nutmeg. Mix well, add 6 oz. (scalded) raisins and 4 oz. blanched almonds sliced into thin strips. Combine lightly with very stiffly beaten 4 egg whites and stuff the pig at once.

Place the cooled roast pig on a dish, decorate with curly kale or myrtle sprigs and in its mouth place either a coloured Easter egg or a slice of horseradish or an intensely yellow lemon.

Next to this, place a sauceboat with Polish Easter sauce or with tartar sauce, which is well known in foreign lands, but which originates from the Polish cuisine.

Polish (Vitamin) Sauce for Easter Meats

Mix 3—4 hard-boiled egg yolks with the juice of 3 lemons into a smooth cream. Thin this down with 1/2 pint thick, slightly sour cream. Add 2—3 bunches of very finely minced chives, 1 heaped teaspoon onion grated to a pulp, some very finely minced parsley sprigs and 1/2 tablespoon freshly grated horseradish.

Salt the sauce to taste, remembering to add a fair-sized pinch of castor sugar. Finally, add 3 finely chopped egg whites (hard-boiled). Part of the cream may be substituted by mayonnaise (1/4 mayonnaise — 3/4 cream).

Make the sauce 2—3 hours before serving, so that it can mature.

This sauce can be served with all cold meats, ham, hard-boiled eggs and fish in aspic, as well as with boiled beef, and not only on Easter.

Horseradish Lithuanian Style

Grate finely a large stick of horseradish (c. 8—10 oz.) and, placing the horseradish on a sieve, pour boiling water over it. In a small pan melt 2 oz. butter, add the horseradish and fry briefly. Add enough sweet cream to make a thick sauce, heat intensely, but do not boil. Add the juice of one lemon, salt and sugar to taste. A raw egg yolk can also be added to the hot sauce. It is best to make horseradish a day earlier.

Ćwikła, a kind of spicy salad made with red beets, has been widely appreciated in Polish kitchens for several ages now. It was the favourite delicacy of the great writer Mikołaj Rej, who was the first eminent writer to abandon the Latin language, widely used in Polish literature until then, and to write in excellent, colourful and expressive Polish. Having acquired a fondness for the Polish language, Rej was also an admirer of Polish food, setting its attractiveness against the foreign, particularly Italian, inventions. He was doubtless keen on cooking himself, which may be seen in his recipe for ćwikła, which is over 400 years old: "Having put the beets in an oven and baked them well, clean them, slice them and place in a cask, add finely grated horseradish, shake, sprinkle with vinegar and season with some salt, so that it is a delicacy in itself... because the juice is tasty and the lady ćwikła herself will be very tasty and will smell very nicely."

Ćwikła
(a red-beet salad with horseradish)

Mikołaj Rej's recipe is still up-to-date, as ćwikła is even today made in the following way:

On a baking-sheet, bake several unpeeled red beets in the oven. They may also be cooked unpeeled, but they are much tastier when baked. Peel the cooled beets and slice very thinly (or use a cabbage-slicer instead of slicing by hand, which requires less work). Pour wine vinegar, thinned down to taste, over the sliced beets. Add 1 tablespoon caraway seeds scalded with boiling water, and 4—5 tablespoons freshly ground horseradish. Ćwikła may of course be soured with lemon juice, adding some (1/2 cup) raw juice of red beets and a glass of dry red wine. Ćwikła made in this way will be exquisite.

Arrange the ćwikła tightly in a glass jar or stoneware pot. The juice should cover the beets two fingers above the surface of the

beets. After two days of maturing in a cool place, the ćwikła develops its full flavour and aroma.

In accordance with tradition, the first day of Easter is spent at home and sometimes the family's closest friends are invited to the Easter table. On the second day we either visit friends (not uninvited of course, although visiting friends once did not call for any invitation), or receive guests. Then cold Easter dishes or *bigos* are served as hors d'oeuvres and after the borsh either a roast or a turkey is served with plenty of trimmings. We close with holiday cakes such as *mazureks* and layer-cakes.

At one time the Tuesday after Easter Sunday was also celebrated as a holiday.

Monday morning was connected with the old custom of pouring water on other people. Hence it was called "Splash Monday". This custom has been preserved until today, especially in villages. Girls were usually the victims of being splashed with water, while the boys were the guileful attackers. The girls defended themselves energetically and noisily. In truth they were pleased, since a girl who was not splashed with water was considered left out on purpose.

In cities water is usually substituted by eau de cologne which is rather sprinkled on the victim than splashed.

Culinary
Report
from 1875

Towards the end of the 19th

century the Old Polish cuisine was modernized and democratized to such an extent that it became the national Polish cuisine in the widest sense of the word, while still retaining the most precious traditions that distinguished it from other nations. Most of the Polish dishes we eat today are not much different from those prepared in the kitchens of our great-grandmothers and grandmothers.

The final version of the Polish cuisine became established in the cities. There were many reasons for this. During the 1846 peasant revolt in Galicia (the Austrian part of Poland) 20 to 90 per cent of the country manors were destroyed, depending on the district, and many of the landowners and their officials were killed. After the brutally suppressed insurrections of 1830—31 and 1863—64, noblemen's estates were confiscated on a mass scale, as a result of which many of the former gentry moved to the cities.

In the cities a patriotic, progressive intelligentsia emerged, which made a permanent contribution to Polish science and art. Those whose aspirations and talents went in other directions filled the ranks of officials required by various Polish institutions.

The intelligentsia was also united by closer social contacts, which may be seen in the example of Warsaw itself. And since Polish hospitality survived all historical disasters, the families that visited each other often sat down to the table together.

The financial situation of the urban intelligentsia was usually not too rosy, though passable, but this did not prevent the continuation of Old Polish culinary traditions; various family and regional recipes were exchanged and adapted to the individual pocket.

The blending of the bourgeois and aristocratic cuisine was a short process, since both culinary styles had been close to each other for some time. The Polish character of Christmas and Easter was particularly emphasized. The partitioning powers could close or open schools of higher learning, repress or tolerate elementary education, carry out various **denationalizing campaigns** — but none of these could weaken national consciousness or patriotism.

The Polish cuisine, which should be praised for its resistance to foreign influence, became, in a way that has perhaps been underestimated by historians, the mainstay of what was Polish in a period of particular difficulties.

Warsaw, even though it was the capital of a country erased from the political map of Europe for over a century, retained its rank of Polish capital in European minds. In other cities, such as Cracow, Lvov and Vilna, a Polish intelligentsia also emerged.

Warsaw continued to attract numerous foreigners along with the greatest virtuosos of those times, with Paganini in the lead. In the foreign press of those times Warsaw was written about often and with an unconcealed sympathy.

The historians of Warsaw culture, Irena and Jan Kosim, recently brought to light an unusually interesting document: eight reports on Warsaw written by Fritz Wernick and published almost simultaneously in the *Danzinger Zeitung* and in Wrocław's *Schlesische Zeitung* in the year 1875. Their great popularity may be seen in the fact that the author included them later in his five-volume work *Städtebilder*.

Wernick's articles were highly esteemed by Bolesław Prus (1845—1912), author of *The Pharaoh*, a novel translated into many languages. He praised them in one of his *Chronicles*, printed in a Warsaw newspaper.

Fritz Wernick (1823—91) was a reporter with an all-round education who had travelled through all of Europe in his search for interesting subjects. Having so much material for comparison at his disposal and possessing the skill of keen observation, he distinguished himself by the great objectivity of his remarks.

Polish food must have made a great impression on him, as we shall see in a moment. From the fragments of his articles that deal with culinary matters, it is safe to assume that he was a connoisseur of good cuisine.

"Warsaw's cuisine," writes Wernick, "has products of excellent quality at its disposal. They are skilfully transformed into exquisite dishes. The food is at the same time extremely concentrated and rich."

After this general statement on Polish culinary characteristics, the author analyzes its virtues and faults in greater detail.

"The nourishing meat of Polish oxen is eaten in considerable quantities here and is inexpensive. The country produces milk on a mass scale, along with butter, eggs and wheat flour of a high quality; the cheeses produced here are excellent."

Nothing but praises so far. But there are not only compliments:

"Warsaw's cuisine only suffers from a lack of good fish. Fish dishes are considered a luxury. Even in the homes there is a small choice of them because the market supplies do not equal the demand. The fish from the Baltic Sea that are brought over in great quantities especially during Lent, rarely reach the table of even wealthy homes. Carp bred in local ponds are eaten with appetite and the slimy taste they acquired in their breeding places does not bother anyone." Everything that concerns sea fish is doubtless true. But the unfavourable comment on carp arouses some doubts. A well prepared carp does not have a "slimy taste", as Polish housewives have known the secret of removing this defect for ages. The most often used and effective method was to keep live carp that was to be eaten in a small bucket for several days, changing the spring water every day. Carp was eaten not because of a lack of other fish, but because it was considered a delicacy, which it was and is if prepared in the right way. There are two famous versions known outside Poland also: "carp Polish style in grey sauce" and "carp Jewish style", both of which appear in cookbooks under the name "carp Polish style". Carp has always been the no. 1 fish in the Polish cuisine. It was bred on a large scale and the invaluable Łukasz Gołębiowski informs us that in ponds near manors: "they were fed malt and potter's clay baked with oil yeast or bread, and they swam over at the sound of the bell, coming up to the surface when the owner or his daughter, who had a fondness for this, rang the bell on the gallery, bringing their favourite food and throwing it with her white hand."

The author of the articles must have either eaten a poorly prepared carp, or, being used to sea-fish dishes, could not appreciate the subtleness and exquisite aroma of this noble fish's flesh. The concentrated character of Polish food was not always a virtue, according to Wernick in 1875, since not every foreigner could digest it well. This appears from his comments which are still relevant, though today we eat much more dietetically and tastier food. But Wernick came in touch with Warsaw cooking over a hundred years ago. "In the Polish cuisine much use is made of fats, strong spices and onions. In the beginning it is not easy to get used to the indigestable, quickly fattening food... Potatoes are usually served mashed with butter, the meat swims in rich sauces; the favourite soup here, composed from meat stock and red beets, prepared with thick, sour cream, is sometimes harmful to the health and calls for a strong stomach."

Thus, the famous Polish borsch made with cream (evidently the author had not eaten clear borsch with *uszka*), which is a light soup compared to the Polish *kapuśniak* (cabbage soup) or *grochówka* (pea soup), did not appeal to the writer's taste.

Compliments appear as well: "Black buckwheat roasted in fat in the manner of the Italian risotto and their *zrazy* made from the finest quality beef sirloin, lightly simmered in a piquant sauce with spices, are incomparably better in taste and have a greater nutritional value than the dish known under the same name in Germany..."

Wernick ate not only in restaurants but, being a guest, he was invited to private homes. It was there that he became acquainted with Polish dishes in their full, authentic charm, since good home-cooking was always superior to restaurant food. Thus, he notes down immediately: "All of these creations of culinary art naturally taste best at a reception in a private home."

This is usually true today as well. But the author finds words of praise for Warsaw restaurants also: "...even medium-class restaurants do not frighten the guest away with poor and tasteless cooking. Everywhere he can count on receiving meat dishes that are tasty and healthy. Restaurants of the first class differ in Warsaw, as everywhere, from the national cuisine."

The last remark could have come from the pen of a contemporary reporter as well, since the "international" cuisine offered by the restaurants of big hotels does suffer from quite a monotonous "culinary cosmopolitism".

When reading Wernick's articles, we admire the accuracy with which the author penetrated Polish culinary characteristics. Moreover, there is no doubt that he did this with a particular fondness. He states, among other things, that in Warsaw he ate plenty of exquisite game and excellent poultry. He writes that poultry is "kept on a great scale in Polish villages". Polish turkey-hens in particular found an enthusiastic admirer in him: "Only in Poland do the choice fat turkeys have an exquisite, unique taste, especially since butter is used unsparingly in roasting, which adds a crispness and saturates the tender meat. Young fattened turkeys can please the most demanding palate and figure on the best menus. This is a real culinary egg of Columbus. Although chicken and goose have been regarded as some of the most exquisite dishes for a long time now, the German cook has never thought of turkey-hens, which are a real feast of flavour when compared with the above mentioned birds."

We do not know what kind of contacts Fritz Wernick made in Warsaw and we do not know the names of the people with whom he usually consorted. But his eyes and ears were most certainly open to everything, thanks to which his Warsaw articles, describing life in the capital in 1875. are a truly valuable document.

Wernick was a frequent visitor of restaurants, as befitted a good journalist. There it was easy to make passing acquaintances and collect up-to-date information. However, he complains that in Warsaw of 1875 A.D. "there is a serious lack of tastefully furnished beerhouses and elegant wine-cellars". He also notices something surprising: "It must be admitted in all fairness that compared with us, drinking for its own sake is not an accepted custom in Warsaw. Wine is drunk here with a meal, usually in restaurants and then the best kinds, especially Hungarian wine which fills Warsaw's cellars to the brims."

Polish beer also merited words of approval:

"In Warsaw beer usually has quite a good reputation... In each restaurant and bigger hotel excellent beer of the best make can be obtained in crystal bottles. It is always served without objections, it is delicious and refreshing. And nowhere is there any animosity towards the guest if he prefers a bottle of beer over wine, each is received equally as this is demanded by the proverbial Warsaw hospitality."

Let us add ourselves: not only Warsaw, but also Polish hospitality.

The busiest places, as Wernick noticed immediately, were Warsaw's confectionery shops, which took the place of reading-rooms, restaurants, or pool-rooms and were favourite meeting places. There were "a great number of these and there are many kinds; they are of various types and of various standards — exquisite and unpretentious, small and spacious; they are very popular and have many customers". We learn that in these confectionery shops coffee, tea, chocolate and bouillon were served. Their regular customers were supplied with all the Polish periodicals and a fine selection of foreign ones, among which Wernick was pleased to find an issue of the *Schlesische Zeitung*. He took a liking to Warsaw pastries at once, showing a particular fondness for the "delicacy worthy of drawing-rooms, the *pączek* (doughnut), which melts in the mouth, this wonderful amalgam of eggs, butter and real cream". Wernick's well-written, spirited and imaginative articles are also read today with great interest, as they give us — though this was not their main purpose — an overall view of the Polish cuisine of the 19th century, with many interesting details. The student of Polish culture and culinary customs will find in them ample and reliable material. They usefully supplement the Polish sources decimated by the last two wars.

The Warsaw cuisine which is described in Wernick's colourful pages was one of the leading European national cuisines and is the direct source of Polish cooking today. One observation that Wernick made causes a certain surprise in the Polish reader: "A complete absence of obesity is common to all circles of Polish society. Among the thousands of inhabitants in Warsaw I did not come across a single fat person, which is all the more curious in that much is eaten here and the food is nourishing."

It is well known that in 1875 a slender figure was valued in women, but we know that this was achieved very often thanks to... corsets. The rest was tactfully covered by long full skirts, quite effectively masking the overweight figure hidden underneath. The "handsome" man of those times, on the other hand, stout and of a solid build, eating "much and nourishing food", was usually slender in his bachelor years. And today, even though we eat with greater restraint and more sensibly, obesity is considered by doctors to be the plague of the 20th century.

Therefore we envy our great grandmothers and great grandfathers for their "complete absence of obesity" so praised by Wernick, which today is not unfortunately so common among men and women "over forty", in spite of the doubtless impressive achievements of contemporary dietetics.

Perhaps the people of those days had a healthier nervous system, which must have been effective in influencing their metabolism.

Polish Recipes
(a selection)

Even the most mouth-water-

ing description cannot replace an actual well-prepared Polish dish. There are different tastes as well as different culinary temperaments. What is reprimanded by some is praised by others as a virtue.

Keeping this well known "culinary truth" in mind, we will now append a series of typically Polish recipes, to be added to the selection of those we have already included in our tale.

Although this book does not exhaust the wealth of achievements and experience of Polish cooking, we would like it to be a source of practical advice for everyday use and for the special occasions of the traditional Polish holidays.

One last remark is needed. The ingredients in the recipes chosen by us have been carefully weighed, but a person more experienced in culinary art and possessing a decidedly individual taste, will perhaps treat them only as loose guidelines. This concerns mostly spices, since some prefer more piquant and aromatic dishes, while others value moderation and discretion in this field. Every good cook has his individual manner and adds all seasonings to taste. It is also possible to limit somewhat the amount of fat, wherever this can be done. However, we advise beginners to stick to the instructions, although the more experienced cooks will sometimes prefer to "interpret" a chosen recipe. Polish food owes to this fondness for individual interpretation its variety, including the considerable number of variants of particularly popular dishes (e.g. of *bigos*, *zrazy*, tripe, *pierogi* etc.).

But for an interpretation to be convincing, the following are needed: experience, imaginative taste and — as in every art — talent.

Boiled Beef Baked in Horseradish Sauce

Cut into thin slices meat cooked in broth, after letting it cool. Arrange the meat on a dish (a shallow oval flame-proof casserole is best) and, having garnished it with the diced vegetables from the broth (this is not necessary), pour over horseradish sauce so that each slice of meat is covered, sprinkle with a teaspoon of butter and bake briefly in the oven until the surface of the sauce browns lightly.

Serve with mashed potatoes with pickles that are peeled and cut into quarters lengthwise. Small freshly salted pickles may be served whole.

Horseradish sauce: Lightly brown 1 oz. flour in 1 1/2 oz. butter, thin this down with a cup of broth (in which the meat has been cooked), adding a small root of grated horseradish (4 tablespoons). Horseradish preserved in vinegar may also be used, but then the amount of lemon juice added to the

sauce should be smaller. Add also 1/2—1
teaspoon sugar. Cook this sauce for 5 minutes and when it thickens add 1/2 cup lightly
soured thick cream blended with 2 raw egg
yolks. Heat the sauce for a moment, mixing
it and not allowing it to boil. Pour the hot
sauce over the meat.

This sauce may also be used for boiled ox
tongue, which is then baked. In that case
tongue stock is used instead of broth.

This manner of serving boiled meat (and
tongue) is very popular in Polish cookery.

Ox Tongue in Grey Sauce

This is one of the traditional Old Polish dishes and holds the rank of a national delicacy. Wash the ox tongue thoroughly several times in warm water and scald it with boiling water, adding vegetables (celeriac and parsley root, carrots, leeks), 1 onion, 5 grains of pepper, 3 grains of pimento (allspice), 1 clove (it may be stuck in the onion) and a small bay leaf. It takes a long time to cook tongue, from 2 to 3 hours, depending on whether the ox was young or elderly.

Remove the skin from the cooked tongue when it cools a little (it comes off very easily) and slice it thinly diagonally.

Grey sauce: Lightly brown 1 oz. flour in 2 oz. butter, thin it down with 3/4 pint tongue stock, add 1/2 cup dry wine, the juice of 1/2 lemon, a piece of thinly sliced lemon rind, and 2 oz. blanched almonds sliced thinly. Colour the sauce with a caramel made from 5 cubes of sugar (moistened in water and lightly browned in a frying-pan). The juice should be mildly sour, spicy with a slight "note" of barely discernible sweetness. Cook the sauce 5 minutes more, place the sliced tongue in it and bring to the boil only once.

Arrange the tongue on a dish and pour sauce over it. Serve the remaining sauce in a sauceboat.

Serve either with mashed potatoes or noodles.

Beef Roast Jewish Style

Pound a neatly cut short piece of roasting meat so that it becomes tender. Salt and leave in a cool place for one hour. Thinly slice 2 cloves of garlic lengthwise and insert into the meat.

In a saucepan or baking-pan heat intensely cooking oil (e.g. soy oil) and, having dusted the meat with flour and ground pepper, fry it on all sides to a fine brown colour. Then place a sliced onion into the pan, add 3—4 tablespoons boiling water and simmer, covered, adding some boiling water from time to time. After about two hours the roast should be tender.

A roast prepared in this manner is very aromatic and tasty. Roasted buckwheat is served with it.

Hussar Roast

Hussar roast was a major adornment of the roast meat repertoire of our grandmothers. Today it has unjustly gone out of fashion somewhat. It is a very tasty dish and a part of the Polish cuisine that deserves to be remembered.

Lightly pound a neatly cut piece of roasting meat (c. 2 lbs.) that is compact in form. Rub with the juice of 1/2 lemon, then allow to rest in a cool place for an hour. Dust the meat with flour and fry in 2 oz. butter until browned on all sides. Pour some boiling water into pan and simmer the meat, covered, for 45 minutes, turning it over from time to time and adding some boiling water.

When the roast is almost tender, place it on a small board and, when it cools somewhat, slice thinly but without cutting right through the meat.

Farce: Simmer 3 medium finely chopped onions in 1—2 oz. butter until tender, not allowing the onions to brown. Add 1 oz. grated whole-wheat bread and salt and pepper to taste. Add 1 raw egg yolk to the slightly cooled farce.

Place the farce into every other slit, form the roast into its previous shape and smooth the surface with a slight pressure.

To the sauce which has formed during roasting in the pan add 1/2—1 oz. flour and a thinly sliced onion. When the onion becomes tender, add 1/2 cup boiling water and the roast, which is then baked, covered, for another 35—40 minutes. Place the whole roast on a dish. Two slices joined by the farce make one portion.

Separately, serve mashed potatoes and sweet cabbage stewed with apples (or tomatoes).

Pork Roast with Caraway
Polish Style

Buy 2 lbs. fine pork, cut into a cube, with the skin. Make shallow incisions in the skin with a sharp knife in a checkerboard pattern. Rub the meat with salt, a large pinch of marjoram and a heaped teaspoon of caraway one hour before roasting.

In a cast-iron pan heat intensely 1 1/2 oz. lard, add meat and brown it on all sides. Place the browned meat with the skin-side down and add 2 sliced onions and some boiling water (or broth, if available). During roasting replenish the evaporated liquid from time to time! After 30 minutes of roasting in a hot oven turn the roast over so that the skin is on top and continue roasting, basting it with its own sauce from time to time. The incisions in the skin will spread out forming an appetizing checkerboard.

Cut the ready roast into thin slices and pour the roast sauce with the onion over it.

Kopytka (a kind of dumpling) from potatoes go very well with this roast, as well as
roasted buckwheat kasha. Sauerkraut stewed with several dried mushrooms and
with 1 tablespoon flour browned in 1 tablespoon lard may also be served.

Kopytka* from Potatoes

Rub 2 lbs. cooked, warm potatoes through a sieve, or put through a meat grinder. Cool the potatoes and beat in 1 large (or 2 small) egg, add about 14—16 oz. flour and salt to taste. Mix, place on a pastry-board dusted with flour and knead to a smooth dough.

Divide the dough into 3—4 parts, form into finger-thick rolls and slice diagonally into small dumplings 1 inch thick. Cook in a large amount of salted boiling water.

Take out the cooked kopytka with a straining spoon and drain well. On a dish pour hot butter or pork fat with cracklings over this. 1 small, very finely chopped onion may be fried in the pork fat.

The kopytka may be cooked a day ahead. Before serving, throw them into boiling salted water and bring to a boil only once. They will be like fresh. They also taste exquisitely if reheated by frying.

*Potato dumplings.

Zrazy

Zrazy are the pride of Old Polish cooking.
The first mention of them was made in the
14th century. It is said that they were one
of the favourite dishes of King Ladislaus
Jagiello. The popularity of Polish zrazy
has survived through the ages until today.
Zrazy are made from tender beef (the so-
called roast meat). The most elegant ones
are made from beef sirloin. There were also
zrazy from lamb and veal, but the classical zrazy are from beef. There are several
kinds of zrazy: the so-called pounded
zrazy and rolled zrazy with various farces.
The most suitable addition to zrazy, which
are usually served in their own sauce, is
roasted buckwheat kasha or pearl barley
kasha.

Rolled Zrazy (Beef Rolls)

Cut well tenderized beef against the grain into not too thin slices, then pound these (take care not to pierce the meat), add salt and pepper and cover with a not too thick layer of farce. After rolling up and tying with a white cotton thread (which has been scalded in boiling water), fry the rolls in butter or pork fat until brown, adding 1 grated onion if desired. Pour 1/2 cup broth over the browned zrazy, cover the saucepan tightly and simmer the rolls over low heat for at least an hour. Add some broth if necessary; two dried mushrooms, a chopped onion and a piece of celeriac cut into strips may be added to the simmering beef rolls. 5 grains pepper, 2 grains pimento (allspice) and a small piece of bay leaf will give the sauce, of which there should be 1/2 pint after cooking, a lightly spicy taste and aroma.

Farce with Horseradish

On a sieve, scald 3 tablespoons freshly grated horseradish with boiling water, drain, brown briefly in one tablespoon butter, remove from heat, add some breadcrumbs and one raw egg yolk, mix thoroughly and salt to taste.

Mushroom Farce

Cook 1 1/2 oz. dried mushrooms in 1/2 pint water, chop finely, brown in butter with a finely chopped onion, add salt and pepper to taste. Roll each piece of beef and then wrap in a thin slice of fresh or smoked pork fat (or bacon). Fry in fat, then simmer, basting with mushroom stock instead of broth. The sauce made this way may be flavoured before serving with 1/4 pint thick sour cream blended with a heaped teaspoon of flour.

Onion Farce

Chop 2 onions finely and simmer in 2 tablespoons butter, but do not brown. Add a tablespoon of sour cream to the simmered onion, along with 1 raw egg yolk and a heaped teaspoon of breadcrumbs. Add salt and pepper to taste.

Sauerkraut Farce

Simmer 10 oz. sauerkraut until tender with 1 tablespoon butter, adding a little boiling water or broth when necessary. Separately, simmer 4 oz. finely diced smoked pork fat (bacon) with 1 thinly sliced onion (which should not brown). Mix the sauerkraut thoroughly with the pork fat and onion, then place the farce on the zrazy.

Polish Farce

Chop 1 peeled firm salt pickle and 5 oz.
pork fat into thin strips about 3 in. long.
Pound the slices of beef, then dust lightly
with salt, spread thinly with mustard, place
3—4 strips of pork fat and a piece of pickle
on each (the pork fat may also be replaced
by bacon) and roll up.

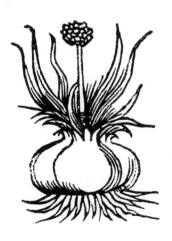

Pounded Zrazy

Pound meat that is carved into portions and form oval zrazy of equal size, then add salt and pepper. Just before frying, dust moderately with flour. Brown the zrazy nicely on both sides, then transfer from the frying pan to a saucepan. Brown 1 thinly sliced onion in the fat remaining in the frying pan, then add the fat and onion to the zrazy. Pour some boiling water or broth over this, then simmer, having added several grains of pepper and 3 grains pimento (allspice), over low heat, covered. If necessary, add some water or broth from time to time.

Pounded zrazy may be simmered with diced vegetables (celeriac and parsley root, carrots, leeks) or 1 oz. dried mushrooms. When tender, flavour the sauce with sour cream to which a teaspoon of flour may be added, then boil briefly. If a glass of dry wine is added instead of cream during the cooking, the zrazy are very tasty.

These few recipes do not exhaust the great many variants that are known in the Polish cuisine. We present one more recipe, written down in 1822 and testifying to the fact that the "legend of Napoleon" reached Polish cooking as well.

Zrazy á la Napoleon

Form oval, not too large zrazy from roasting beef (2—3 lbs). Add salt and pepper, dust with flour and fry in butter without browning.

Shred (not too finely) 2 whole carrots, 2 parsley roots, 1/2 medium celeriac, 1 kohlrabi, and 1 large onion.

In a saucepan melt 2 copious tablespoons of butter. Place the vegetables into this and the zrazy on the vegetables. Add alternate layers of meat and vegetables with vegetables as the last layer. Cover the whole with a glass of white wine, cover the saucepan tightly and seal with dough, place in a larger saucepan with boiling water and cook over low heat 2 1/2 hours. The wine may be substituted with mushroom stock, but wine makes them more piquant.

Old Polish cuisine was famous for its exquisite hams and *kiełba-sas*, known already in the Slavic cuisine. *Kiełbasas* were served in various ways, hot and cold, fried and roasted, with cabbage and peas and in sauce. In the 17th century a good cook in a noble-man's house had to show his skill by making *kiełbasas* in a dozen different ways, while an aristocratic cook had to know 24 ways! One of the favourites was *kiełbasa* cut into slices and served with a hot, piquant sauce. It was eaten with a spoon during the reign of **Augustus II** and **Augustus III**.

Kiełbasa in Polish Sauce

This is a simple but tasty dish and if we serve it with mashed potatoes, it can constitute a complete dinner course.

Pour a bottle of light beer and an equal amount of water over 1 1/2—2 lbs. fresh ("white") kiełbasa or lightly smoked kiełbasa (e.g. "serdelowa"). Add 2 finely diced large onions and cook, covered, for 20 minutes. Put the broth through a sieve and mix thoroughly with 1 tablespoon flour browned in 1 tablespoon butter. Add 2 tablespoon wine vinegar (or lemon juice to taste) to the sauce, along with a scant tablespoon of sugar and salt to taste. A teaspoon of the liquid seasoning used for sauces may also be added. Bring the sauce to a boil and into it place the kiełbasa, cut into pieces diagonally.

The kiełbasa may also be served in a spicily seasoned onion or tomato sauce. Frankfurters may also be served in a traditional Polish beer, onion or tomato sauce.

Chicken Polish Style

For making chicken Polish style, one must choose really young medium-sized chickens. Two chickens are necessary for four persons. Frozen ones may also be used although fresh birds are preferable.

Wash the birds briefly but thoroughly (especially inside) in cold water, dry with a clean cloth, salt moderately, fill with farce, sew up the opening and roast.

Stuffing: Soak 1 dried white roll in cold milk and squeeze out well. Cream 2 oz. butter with 1 raw egg yolk until fluffy, add the roll, a heaped teaspoon of very finely minced parsley (a teaspoon of minced dill may also be added), mix thoroughly, salt moderately and mix gently with 1 beaten egg white. If the stuffing seems too thin, some breadcrumbs may be added. This amount of stuffing is enough for 1 medium chicken.

If there is a liver in one of the chickens, then mix the raw liver, chopped to a pulp, with butter and egg yolk.

During the roasting braise the chicken
liberally with butter, then with its own
sauce. When done and browned, cut lengthwise into halves, place on a dish and
sprinkle with the sauce that has formed
while roasting, serving the rest of the sauce
in a sauceboat.

A classical addition to chicken Polish style
is cucumber salad or lettuce seasoned in a
way typical to Polish cooking, with sour
cream, along with young potatoes with
butter and dill.

Lettuce Polish Style

Divide 1—2 heads of crisp lettuce into leaves. Wash the leaves, then dry in a clean cloth.

Prepare the salad dressing from thick, fresh, not too sour cream, adding some lemon juice, sugar and salt to taste.

Just before serving, place the leaves (whole) in a salad bowl, pour the cream over them, mix gently with two forks so that they are evenly covered with the dressing and decorate the salad with hard-boiled egg quarters. Whoever likes garlic may rub the salad bowl with a garlic clove before placing the lettuce in it.

Mizeria* Polish Style

It is difficult to establish today why this delicious and refreshing cucumber salad has been given the rather gloomy name**.

Peel thinly young cucumbers with small seeds and shred them thinly. Sprinkle with a teaspoon of salt and squeeze out lightly after a few minutes.

The dressing is made with cream in the same way as for lettuce — for each 1/2 cup sour cream add the juice of 1/2 lemon, 1/2 teaspoon castor sugar and, if necessary, a little salt and a copious teaspoon of finely minced dill. Dust the mizeria with 1/4 teaspoon ground pepper. Mix and place in a cool place half an hour before serving.

---

* Cucumber Salad.
**Mizeria, from Lat. *miseria*, in Eng. *misery*.

We have been unable to pinpoint the moment when turkey appeared on Polish tables. It did happen quite early, however, probably in the first half of the 15th century during the reign of King Casimir Jagiellon, since in those days noblemen's sabres were called "turkeys" on account of their bent shape.

Turkey meat (young hen turkeys are even more delicate and tasty) is a great and expensive delicacy. Turkey may be served in various ways, also cold and in aspic, but hot roasted turkey is probably the best. It has been one of the most elegant dishes on the Polish table for a long time, served relatively seldom, and therefore a great treat.

Roasted Double-Stuffed Turkey

Among the many different ways of serving turkey, double-stuffed turkey Polish style deserves special praise.

Prepare the turkey for roasting, salt it and, if desired, rub with lemon juice (remember to remove the tendons from the thighs!) and stuff with two different farces 2 hours before serving. Fill the crop with one of these (sew up after filling) and the body with the other.

Stuffing for the crop: Chop the turkey liver to a pulp (which may also be put through a metal sieve, if desired) and mix with a copious tablespoon of butter and 2 raw egg yolks, adding 2—4 oz. small raisins, 2 tablespoons breadcrumbs and to taste: pepper, nutmeg, 1—2 cloves ground to a powder and salt. Mix this gently with very stiffly beaten 2 egg whites and fill the crop with it.

Stuffing for turkey: Chop finely 1 medium onion and simmer until tender in 1 oz. butter without letting it brown. Cut 4 oz. fresh pork fat into not too small cubes. Soak 4 anchovies briefly, clean and remove the bones (they may easily be substituted with a level tablespoon of anchovy paste). Soak 2 dried white rolls with the crust grated off in milk and squeeze out well. Cut 1 lb. cold roast veal into cubes. Put all the

above mentioned ingredients 2—3 times
through a meat grinder with 1 tablespoon
drained capers and the sauce (jelly) from the
roast. Beat in 3 whole eggs, add 4 oz. melted butter, pepper and salt (and a pinch of
nutmeg if desired) to taste. Stuff the bird
with this farce, having mixed it well by
hand.

Place the turkey in a deep pan, pour butter
over it liberally and roast in a medium hot
oven 2—3 hours, or longer if the turkey is
very large. If the breast browns too quickly,
cover it with aluminium foil and remove the
foil when the thighs are done.

Arrange the turkey, divided in the usual
manner, surrounding it with the farce, cut
into slices. Both farces may be placed alternately or separately. Just before serving,
sprinkle the meat with the sauce which has
formed in the pan and serve the rest of the
(hot!) sauce in a sauceboat.

Separately, cranberry preserves may be
served. They go very well with the turkey
meat as well as with both farces.

Gołąbki*

Gołąbki are one of the most popular, simple and very tasty dishes on the Polish table. They are seasoned differently in different regions, but the principle remains the same: the farce is rolled up in cabbage leaves. The inexpensive and delicious gołąbki may be prepared in somewhat larger quantities, since they are even better when reheated in a pot or refried in butter or lard.

Cut out the cabbage stump deeply, then place the head of the cabbage (it should not be too firm) into boiling water and cook for 15—20 minutes. When it cools a little, gently divide into individual leaves. Set aside the four outer leaves, as they are too hard and usually damaged, and use them for lining the pot.

* Stuffed cabbage.

Gołąbki with Rice and Mushrooms

In a large amount of salted water cook 8—10 oz. rice until almost tender, rinse with cold water and drain on a sieve. Cook 2 oz. dried mushrooms and chop finely, reserving the stock. Chop finely 2 medium onions and brown lightly in 2 oz. butter (or lard). Mix the above mentioned ingredients, add salt and pepper to taste. 1 whole raw egg may also be added, in which case the stuffing will be firmer.

Place the farce on each cabbage leaf (pound the thick, main "nerve" of the leaf with a knife handle lightly, which makes rolling up easier), fold the edges of the leaf over the farce and roll up the gołąbek tightly.

Arrange the gołąbki tightly in a stoneware or thick enameled pot, which has been lined with cabbage leaves. Pour salted mushroom stock over them, add some boiling water so that the gołąbki are barely covered with liquid, cover the pot and bake the gołąbki in an oven. Instead of the stock, rye borsch (żur) may be used over the gołąbki. The stock may then be used for making the sauce (flour browned in butter with soured cream), which is served with the baked gołąbki.

Gołąbki are tastiest when baked a day ahead (in an oven) and quickly reheated in the same pot the next day. Gołąbki with mushrooms and rice are sometimes served as a Christmas dish.

Gołąbki with Rice and Meat

Cook 8—10 oz. rice as in the recipe above. Mushrooms may be added, but they are not necessary. Grind 10 oz. cooked pork and add to the rice with 1 large onion, simmered in 2 oz. butter (lard) and, if desired, 1 raw egg.

Proceed as in the recipe above.

Note: instead of pork, 10 oz. ground kiełbasa or finely chopped ham may be added to the rice. The baked gołąbki may be fried in pork fat if desired and sprinkled with the melted pork fat and cracklings. Separately, mushroom sauce may be served with them, or a concentrated tomato sauce.

Gołąbki Country Style

In the older days, in the villages especially, whole heads of sauerkraut were used in making gołąbki. Today sauerkraut made of whole cabbages is very rare, so that country-style gołąbki are also rolled up in sweet cabbage leaves.

Grate finely 2 lbs. raw, peeled potatoes and when they let out their juice, pour it away, adding 14 oz. cooked and mashed potatoes to the raw potatoes, 2 finely chopped onions simmered in 2—3 oz. lard, 2 oz. raw buckwheat kasha and salt and pepper to taste. Mix the farce thoroughly, place on cabbage leaves, roll up and arrange the gołąbki tightly in a pot. Pour salted water over them, cook over low heat for 15 minutes and bake, covered, in an oven.

Refry in lard the following day. This authentically peasant inexpensive version of gołąbki is delicious.

Pierogi, a dish which most likely comes from the older Slavic folk cuisine, has acquired great long-lasting popularity in Polish kitchens in villages as well as in cities.

Pierogi are an inexpensive, easy to make, nourishing and very tasty dish. They may be served directly after cooking, or fried when cool. In both versions they are delicious, so that it is worthwhile making them in greater quantities, served freshly cooked for lunch and refried for dinner.

Pierogi*
Dough for Pierogi

On a pastry board knead dough from 14 oz. flour, a pinch of salt and a whole egg, adding some lukewarm water in order to get a quite loose dough which is very well kneaded and does not stick to the hands or pastry board. Divide the dough (covered with a bowl so that it does not dry) into 4 parts, then roll each one out thinly. With a tea-cup or wine-glass cut out circles that are 2—2 1/2 in. in diameter. Place a heaped teaspoon of the filling on each circle, fold over and press the edges firmly so that

---
* Dumplings.

it does not open during cooking. The shaping of pierogi itself calls for a little experience, as they should be neat, not crushed, well filled and well stuck together at the edges.

Various Fillings

1) For *Russian pierogi* (especially popular in Little Poland) put 1 lb. cooked potatoes and 6 oz. cottage cheese through a meat grinder. Add 1 small raw egg to this, along with 1 medium onion, finely chopped and browned to a golden brown. Add salt and pepper to taste. Cook the shaped pierogi in a shallow wide pot, in a large amount of lightly salted water. When they come up to the surface, cook them over low heat for 4—5 minutes more, then take them out with a large strainer spoon and drain well. Place them on a dish. These are the standard steps in the preparation of all pierogi. Pour butter or pork fat (with cracklings) over the Russian pierogi. Separately, thick, lightly soured cream may be served.

2) Pierogi with a farce made from *sweet cabbage* or *sauerkraut* are very popular. Cook a sweet cabbage (2 lbs.) in salted water, chop finely and simmer until tender in butter or lard with 1 medium finely chopped (or previously browned) onion. Add salt and pepper to taste. Several cooked dried mushrooms with the stock may be added to the cabbage, after which it is fried for a while, so that the filling is thick enough. The farce is tasty even without the mushrooms. Some add 1 finely chopped hard-boiled egg to the farce.

In the case of sauerkraut, take 2 lbs. of it, very finely chopped, and simmer in 2 oz. fat (pork fat or butter), adding a fried onion, pepper and salt and some breadcrumbs. Cooked, very finely chopped mushrooms may also be added, using the stock to flavour a soup.

Pierogi made with sweet cabbage are served with hot (but not browned) butter and those made with sauerkraut are served with pork fat and cracklings.

3) Pierogi with cheese: rub c. 1 lb. well drained cottage cheese through a wire sieve, then mix thoroughly with 1 small egg and salt moderately. The filling swells during cooking, so do not use too much. Serve immediately after cooking, after pouring butter (2 oz.) liberally over them. Separately, sour cream may be served. These pierogi should not be reheated.

4) *Pierogi with meat.* This is a valued dinner dish in the Polish cuisine, and is served with various vegetable salads, and especially raw sauerkraut. The filling is made from 1 lb. cooked beef, ground together with a soaked and squeezed out white roll (2 oz.), seasoned with 1 medium, finely chopped onion, lightly browned in 1 1/2 oz. butter, pepper and salt. If the filling is too dry, add 1 raw egg yolk. Usually melted pork fat with cracklings is poured over the meat pierogi or else browned dry breadcrumbs and melted butter. They are also very good when refried (lightly browned).

5) *Pierogi with buckwheat kasha*. This is an authentically folk version of pierogi, worth mentioning as it is very tasty. Dry roast 1 cup buckwheat kasha, add 1 finely chopped onion which has been browned in pork fat or butter (2 oz. fat), add salt and pepper to taste. 4 oz. cottage cheese rubbed through a wire sieve may be added to the filling. Butter or pork fat with cracklings is poured over pierogi with kasha and sour cream is served.

6) *Sweet pierogi with cheese*. These are a typically Polish and very nourishing dessert, which should be remembered when composing a dinner menu to which they will be an attractive addition.

The dough is prepared in a slightly different manner from that of the previously mentioned pierogi. It is made from 1 lb. flour, 1 1/2 oz. butter, 1 whole egg, 1 egg yolk, about 1/2 cup lukewarm water and a pinch of salt.

The filling: mix 1 lb. cream cottage cheese

that has been put through a sieve with
2—3 oz. sugar. Add 1 tablespoon very
finely diced candied orange peel and 2 oz.
small raisins.
Pour butter liberally over the cooked pierogi and, separately, serve fresh thick,
slightly sour cream. These exquisite pierogi
should not be reheated.

7) *Pierogi with blueberries*, sour or sweet
cherries, diced apples or very thick preserves, are made in the dough used for Russian
pierogi. The sour and sweet cherries may be
stoned. The fruit is mixed with 1 tablespoon
sifted breadcrumbs and 1 tablespoon sugar.
Separately, sugar and sour cream are served
with pierogi with fruit, over which butter
has been poured.

Kołaczyki* with Onion

Kołaczyki with onion are an exquisite side dish which is served before soup. They taste just as good when served "straight from the oven" with tea, instead of a sweet baba or cakes.

First, make the yeast dough from 12 oz. wheat flour, 1/2 oz. yeast, 1/4 cup luke-warm milk, 1 1/2 oz. butter, 2 raw egg yolks and 1/3 teaspoon salt. The dough should be kneaded well, until it does not stick to the bowl or to your hands. Of course the dough may be kneaded with the aid of an electric mixer, in which case it will be just as tasty. When the dough rises to twice its size, shape into small buns, each weighing c. 1 oz. Arrange these on a butter-ed baking sheet, two inches apart. After 30—45 minutes, when the buns rise, make small holes by pressing down with fingers. Spread egg white over them and place onion farce in the hollows.

* Cake.

Filling for kołaczyki: Scald 8 oz. thinly sliced onions with boiling water, on a sieve, and drain thoroughly. Simmer until tender, without browning it, in 2 oz. butter. Season the simmered onions with 1/2 teaspoon sugar and a generous pinch of ground pepper.

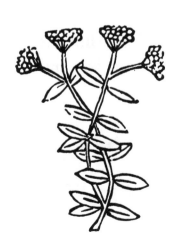

Kołaczyki with Cabbage

These are just as attractive as kołaczyki with onion. They are served warm, "straight from the oven" with soups or with tea.
The dough is made as in the previous recipe.

The filling: Divide a small head of sweet cabbage into quarters, cook for 15 minutes, cool a little, chop very finely and fry in 2 oz. lard along with a finely chopped medium onion. Add salt and pepper to taste and 2 oz. grated cheese (lightly dried), or 2 oz. finely crumbled goat cheese and 1 raw egg. After mixing all the ingredients well, place the filling into the hollows in the buns, spread with lightly beaten egg and bake in a medium hot oven, taking care they do not brown too much.

*Warsaw Pączki**

Pączki that are carefully made precisely according to this recipe are superior to even the best confectioner's pączki. However, the recipe is not inexpensive and is not for young housewives who are taking their first steps in the noble art of cooking. The art of frying pączki also takes up a lot of time and if they are to be served on New Year's Eve (they must be still lukewarm!), their preparation must be begun in the early afternoon hours.

Begin with the preparation of the yeast by dissolving 2—2 1/2 oz. of it in milk (about 1/3 cup), along with 4 oz. flour and 1 tablespoon sugar. When the yeast rises enough, add 1 lb. flour, 8 egg yolks creamed with 3 oz. sugar, about 1/2 pint barely lukewarm sweet cream (heated only, but not boiling), ground vanilla (1/2 bean) sifted through a dense sieve, 6 oz. melted lukewarm butter, 1/3 teaspoon salt and a glass of

* Doughnuts.

spirit. Some very finely grated lemon rind may also be added.

Knead the dough well by hand; when it does not stick to the hands or bowl, it is ready. It should not be too thick, but shiny and springy. When it starts to rise again, take out c. 1 1/2 oz. portions with a tablespoon (it is best to weigh each one, so that the pączki will be of equal size), shape into small circles by hand, place 1/2 teaspoon filling in the middle, fold over and shape into a ball. Place with the join underneath on a cloth dusted with flour. Cover the pączki with a clean cloth. When they expand to almost twice their size, gently remove the flour with a small brush or feather. Fry them in portions in intensely heated lard, in shallow and wide saucepan so that they float freely in the fat without touching each other. In order to avoid excessive browning, 2—3 slices of raw potato may be added to the hot lard, or 1—2 tablespoons water may be added from time to time.

When the pączki brown underneath, turn them over gently. When done, take them out carefully (e.g. in a wide horsehair sieve or on white blotting-paper), drain off the fat and, while still warm, dust liberally with castor sugar with ground sifted vanilla. Lukewarm pączki may be iced with a thin punch icing and the moist icing sprinkled with very finely chopped candied orange peel.

The classical filling for Polish pączki are well-drained rose hip preserves mixed with very finely chopped, or preferably ground almonds. For this recipe the filling must be made from 6 oz. lightly heated ground rose hip preserve (weigh after draining off the excess syrup!) and 3 oz. ground (blanched) almonds.

Index

Sauces

Soups

Fish

Meat (Including Poultry and Game)

Beef

Egg Dishes

Vegetable and Mushroom Dishes

Kashas, Noodles, Dumplings, etc.

Cakes

Desserts